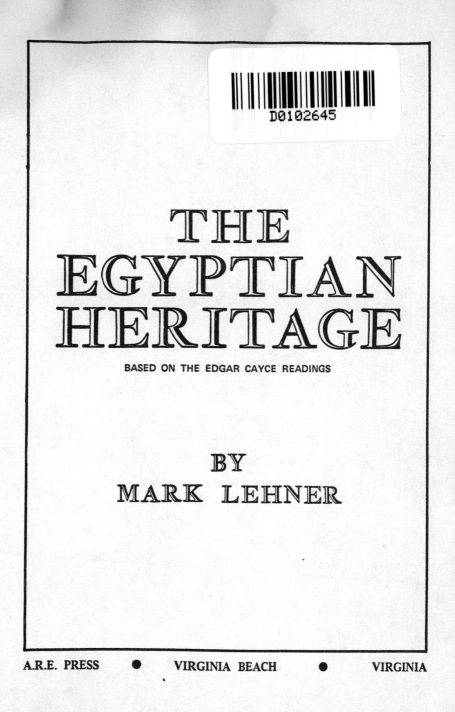

THE EGYPTIAN HERITAGE

BASED ON THE EDGAR CAYCE READINGS

BY
MARK LEHNER

A.R.E. PRESS • VIRGINIA BEACH • VIRGINIA

Dedicated to my mother
ETHEL LOIS LEHNER

Special thanks to Robert Hawk
And thank you, Violet Shelley and Ann Clapp

Copyright © 1974
by the
Edgar Cayce Foundation

ISBN 87604-071-7

8th Printing, October, 1981

Printed in U.S.A.

CONTENTS

PREFACE

There are 1,159 Edgar Cayce readings which contain references and information on the Ra Ta period in Egypt. The story presented here has been culled from approximately 300 of these readings. This number includes all those readings which deal extensively with the subject.

In weaving the Ra Ta story from these hundreds of readings, personal interpretation and selection by the author could not be avoided. Certain problems concerning the sequence of events occasionally arose. I cannot say that the order of events presented here is *exactly* in accord with what actually transpired in that distant period, or what the source of the readings intended to present. This is due to minor variations in the readings themselves pertaining to certain dates and names of places.

The consistency of the readings in hundreds of references to this Egyptian period vastly outweighs any variations, however. Even in regard to very specific details, the consistency of the readings is remarkable. In any case, I have endeavored to remain as free from personal interpretation as possible — letting the readings themselves tell the story.

In presenting correlative Egyptological data I will attempt to demonstrate that there are good empirical reasons for believing that the Ra Ta story is, in fact, rooted in truth. Of course, the final confirmation lies beneath the paws of the Sphinx at Giza.

A final word. If the reader finds the readings' language awkward at times, or a bit archaic, I offer this explanation from the source.

> This aside: The interpreting of these records, to be sure, is not from English — neither is it from the Egyptian language of the present day, but rather from the language that the entity's people brought into the land — not Sanskrit, not the early Persian; though the peoples came from that land which is a part of Iran or Carpathia.   1100-26

INTRODUCTION

Academic Egyptology (the study of Egypt as taught by modern archaeology, texts, and history professors) informs us that the pageantry of human experience in dynastic Egypt encompassed a span of four thousand years.

From the earliest known predynastic cultures and the First Dynasty of Menes (3,400 B.C.) until the birth of Christ, temples, monuments, whole cities were built and put to ruin, leaving us powerful names of the times inscribed in royal cartouches: Zoser, Khufu, Amenemhet, Thutmose, Amenhotep, Ahknaten, Rameses, Cleopatra. Priests and monarchs vied for power; the great gods rose in stature, then dwindled to a faded memory: Amon, Ra, Ptah, Thoth, Osiris, Isis, Aten, Anubis, and Set. Cycles of unity and division, strength and weakness, plenty and poverty, opulence and oppression, make up this 4,000-year dynastic period.

The source of the material presented here is not scientific, i.e., based on archaeology or history but psychic, as the distinction is now made. Our story has been pieced together from over 1,100 "life readings" given to people by Edgar Cayce while in an unconscious state. Our focus goes far beyond the beginning of the Nile society as given in academic history through 5,000 years of historical vacuity to 10,500 B.C. It is encompassed by the Ra Ta story, for Ra Ta, the high priest of those times, is the central character in the drama presented by the readings.

The story is not one only of heroes and demi-gods, pomp and grandeur — nor merely a mythical sort of fantasy. A careful scrutiny of the Cayce readings reveals intimate human passions, love and enmity, suffering and disgrace, grace and inspiration.

One way to view Egyptian history is as a mandala of human experience. A mandala is the basic symbol or archetype of existence; in its simplest form, a circle with its center. As an image, the mandala is a way of viewing any experience holistically. Peripheral phenomena are motivated from the center or essence of the experience. And as every mandala — whether atom, galaxy, or historical cycle — motivates from its nucleus, we direct our attention there to gain an understanding of its essence.

If the readings' story of 10,500 B.C. approaches truth (it is the author's premise that it does on several levels of significance) then we should consider seriously the implications of this epoch being the motivating center of the Egyptian Mandala — the real legacy of Ancient Egypt. As such it would be a legacy increasingly obscured in the later dynasties, which, in their science, religion, and art forms were only echoing those earlier events that gave impetus to their culture and cosmology.

According to the readings, it is a legacy which will soon be rediscovered, and will bear profound determinations — not only for the history of dynastic Egypt, but for the entire physical and spiritual epic of our evolution on this planet, up to the present, and for the years yet to pass.

Before the narrative of the Ra Ta period begins, however, we should extend our sense of history even further than 10,500 B.C. — to over ten *million* years ago . . .

Part One

THE RA TA STORY

Chapter One

THE HOMELAND

Prologue

The period in the world's existence from the present time being ten and one-half million [10,500,000] years, and the changes that have come in the earth's plane many have risen in the lands. Many lands have disappeared . . . 5748-2

The earliest human activity in the Nile Valley presented in the readings is a fade-in on a dimly-lit primeval convention of wise men occurring 10,500,000 years ago.

The world's geography in this misty period was very different from today:

The man's indwelling was then in the Sahara and the upper Nile regions, the waters then entering the now Atlantic from the Nile region rather than flowing northward; the waters in the Tibet and Caucasian entering the North Sea; those in Mongolia entering the South Seas; those in the cordilleras entering the Pacific; those in the plateau entering the Northern Seas . . . and the first ruler of groups set self in that place in the upper Nile, near what is now known as the Valley of Tombs.

In the second rule there came peace and quietude to the peoples, through the manner of the ruler's power over the then known world forces . . . then that ruler set about to gather those wise men from the various groups to compile those as that ruler felt the necessary understanding to all peoples for the indwelling of the Divine Forces to become understood and to break away from the fear of the animal kingdom then overrunning the earth. 5748-1

The purpose of the convention, then, seems twofold: an organized attempt at collective self-preservation against a threatening animal kingdom, and a correlating of truths and understandings concerning human relationship to a Higher Being.

Then, as these were gathered from the five nations, we find the subjects of those pertaining to manifestations of the development of man and man's ability to cope with the conditions, and the forces wherein men were given their supremacy over the other conditions in the earth's plane. And the first as was given by the ruler was, then, that the force that gives man, in his weak state, as it were, the ability to subdue and overcome the great beasts that inhabit the plane of man's existence must come from a higher source. Hence the first law of self-preservation in the physical plane attributed to Divine or Higher Forces . . . yet there were many men of giant stature to meet the conditions as seen, yet the approach of that same force to some was reached through the power, heat, significance of Sun's force, of Moon's wane, of waters bringing forth all manners of organisms necessary for developments in the plane.   5748-3

The numbers of the people that came together for the purpose then numbering some forty and four [44].
The Courts as were made were in the tents and the caves of the dwellers of the then chosen priest from the Arabian or Tibetan country, who came as one among those to assist with the astrologer and the soothsayers of the desert of now the eastern and western worlds, and with this the conclave was held for many, many moons.   5748-2

According to the readings, the Egyptian *Book of the Dead,* considered by scholars to be one of the oldest religious texts, owes its birth to this primeval gathering of minds.

The first laws, then, partook of that of the study of self, the division of mind, the division of the solar systems, the division of man in the various spheres of existence through the earth plane and through the earth's solar system. *The Book of the Dead,* then, being the first of those that were written as the inscribed conditions necessary for the development in earth or in spirit planes.   5748-2

These "first laws as regarding the indwelling of Higher Forces in the earth's plane" (5748-3) were recorded at that time. The readings tell us that even these records may yet be found and give their approximate location:

With the absence of the communications as is given, this was written on tables of stone and slate, with the characters of same. In the first of the pyramids built in the Valley of the Shadow, there still may be found unto this day portions of data as was preserved with the ruler, who afterward was worshiped as the representative of God made manifest in earth. These will be found in the northwest corner or chamber of this mound.   5748-4

The events surrounding this apparent genesis of Egyptian culture became hidden both beneath the surface of the earth and in the collective unconscious. There they would be recovered an eon or more later, by archaeologists searching the past, at a time still beyond the periphery of modern memory.

Until then, during the vast intervening expanse of time, the world-spirit was to give way to the advanced civilization of Atlantis. This would be a dominant influence in the planet for hundreds of thousands of years.

World Setting — Atlantis

The time is around 10,500 B.C., a period which academic history designates as "Upper Paleolithic II." This means that the central technological achievement of humans at this time was the use of stone implements.

What is the world setting — the spirit of this age, given in the readings? 200,000 years of Atlantean grandeur were coming to a close, for that great continent, already broken up into islands, was entering the final stage of its phased destruction — owing to the misuse of power by its inhabitants.

> . . . the entity was in the land that has been called the Atlantean, during those periods when there was the breaking up of the land and there had been the edict that the land must be changed. 315-4

> . . . the entity was in the Atlantean experience when there was the breaking up of the land itself, through the use of *spiritual* truths for the material gains of physical power. 1152-1

This was a time of high energies, a completion of a grand cycle with the ensuing destructive and creative forces prevalent when one age dies to give birth to another. For even as Atlantis released its dying breaths, a great division inherent in that culture since its inception was causing strife and turmoil. The Sons of the Law of One, those who followed tenets relating to a Higher Being, and the Sons of Belial, those who followed self-interest and gratification, were still at odds in these final moments of Atlantis.

> In that sojourn, then, we find that Assen-ni was of the children of the Law of One; with the children of Belial as the negative influence or force among the children of men.
> And there was the realization by Assen-ni that those who had been born were through no fault of their own being used as creatures for exploitation; and that through the very influence and power of the children of Belial the Creative Energies were being used for destructive purposes — or as cloaks behind which their activities might be carried on. 1007-3

The readings go so far as to suggest that it was this conflict itself which caused the destruction of the continent.

> . . . the entity was in the Atlantean land, during those periods when there were those activities that brought about the last destruction of same

5

through the warrings between the children of the Law of One and the
Sons of Belial . . . 1599-1

Yet, many Atlanteans were aware of the coming destructions and
issued warnings. A great migration was under way.

With the realization of the children of the Law of One that there was
to be the final breaking up of the Poseidian-Atlantean lands, there were the
emigrations with many of the leaders to the various lands. 1007-3

The entity was among those who journeyed to other lands, knowing
much of the activities of the Sons of Belial as well as the precautions and
warnings that had been issued by the children of the Law of One. 1604-1

Many of the immigrants journeyed to the Americas — Yucatan,
Peru, Ecuador, Mexico, and Ohio. Others went to the Pyrenees and
portions of western Europe. And some of these technologically
advanced and powerful peoples found their way into the Nile Valley.

. . . the entity was in the Egyptian land, as now called.
There the entity was among those who were the Atlanteans that came
into Egypt. 1574-1

. . . the entity was in that land now known as the Egyptian, during those
periods when there were the incomings of those from other lands for those
activities that were begun by the Priest there.
The *entity* was a sojourner from Atlantis, or from the temple in
Poseidia. 961-1

Origins — The Caucasus

As all endings are necessarily beginnings, we must shift our focus
from the turbulent close of the Atlantean Age to the beginnings of a
new era, originating with a tribal people northeast of Egypt in the
Caucasian Mountains.

The readings describe what was to develop when this tribe entered Egypt as "one of the most momentous occasions or periods in
the world's history . . . " (900-275)

. . . for as has been given, there are many in the present earth's plane
that experienced many of the changes — pro and con — during the
Egyptian sojourn, that meant so much to the history of the human race
from that period to the present . . . 341-24

The religious leader of this tribe was one named Ra Ta. In a reading
concerning his life we are told:

. . . there are many peoples, even nations, that were influenced by the
material activities of the entity in that experience. 294-147

Ra Ta, it seems, was not one of these Caucasians. The readings

6

refer to him as being from a "people of Zu" (Sumer?). Apparently, his birth — his life — was a special circumstance, for Ra Ta "was the son of a daughter of Zu that was *not* begotten of man." (294-147)

In joining with these Caucasians, called the "people of Ararat" after their ruler, Ra Ta was not accepted immediately. Inter-group prejudice was a condition he had to meet.

> In the entrance, then, he came rather as one that was rejected by those peoples about him . . . [and] there was brought to those peoples of Zu's the condemnation of those of Ararat, who had established what would now be called a *community* home in the land later known as Ararat, or where the flood later brought those peoples who again joined with many in peopling the earth after that destruction which was caused by those changes in the land known as Og.
>
> The entity then grew in grace with the peoples by the manner of [his] conduct . . .   294-147

What sort of man was Ra Ta, and what potentials marked him for a special destiny? The readings describe him as one of vision and clairvoyance — a channel for what is termed repeatedly as the Creative Energies.

We should hasten to recognize, however, that many individuals of that period were of a different physical, mental and spiritual constitution than is common today.

> Ye say, then, such an entity was a god! No. No — ye only say that because there is the misunderstanding of what were the characters or types of spiritual evolution as related to *physical* evolution in the earth at that period.
>
> As an illustration (this merely illustrating, now): It is hard for an individual, no matter how learned he may be, to conceive of the activities that exist only three miles above the earth. Why? Because there are no faculties within the individual entity in the present *capable* of conceiving that which is not represented within his individual self.
>
> Yea — but the individual of that period was not so closely knit in matter. Thus the activities of the realms of relativity of force, relativity of attraction in the universe, *were* an experience of the souls manifesting in the earth at that period, see?   281-43

But Ra Ta was considered exceptionally gifted even for that period, "a man then of unusual abilities as well as appearance and manners of conduct." (294-147) But however exalted his abilities may have been, the readings reveal a sense of humility in his character, as one among many in search of spiritual understanding.

> Thus we find that the experiences of individuals of the period, seeking for the understanding as to the evolution of the souls of men, might be

7

compared to the minds of individuals in the present who are seeking an understanding as to man's use of physical or atomical structure in his own relationships.

Then, the individual of that experience or period was not necessarily one other than a soul or entity seeking the knowledge as to the relationship of that which would sustain and gain *for* man the abilities not only to continue the physical evolution but the spiritual or soul evolution as well.

Such an one, then, was Ra — or Ra Ta.
(Study this, or you won't understand it!)   281-42

From an overview of his activities in this entire period, we must conclude that Ra Ta's distinguishing talent was the ability to *apply* spiritual understanding to basic human needs, encompassing home, marriage, law and ethics, healing, and science.

Ra Ta knew Egypt was the place for the implementation of his ideals and visions:

Why Egypt? This had been determined by that leader or teacher (not physical leader, but spiritual interpreter or guide) as the center of the universal activities of nature, as well as the spiritual forces, and where there might be the least disturbance by the convulsive movements which came about in the earth through the destruction of Lemuria, Atlantis, and — in later periods — the flood.

What were the factors, ye ask, which determined this in his mind? or from what concept did the entity gain that knowledge? Was it just a concept, just a revelation, just a physical analysis, or what? . . .

Then, there were the mathematical, the astrological and the numerological indications, as well as the individual urge.   281-42

At the age of twenty-one Ra Ta prophesied that the people of Ararat would enter Egypt so that a spiritual understanding might be merged with an advanced material standard of living.

In this period, then, there was the prophecy by Ra Ta that the son of Ararat [Arart] was to journey into this land where there was then the higher state of developments as to the necessities, and those abilities to enjoy and enjoin the activities of the mental and material bodies in their associated actions.   294-147

Q-7. What was the climatic condition of the country at this time?
A-7. More fertile than even in the present with the overflow as occurs, for only about a third of the present Sahara was there, though it was sandy loam with silt — in the use of the agricultural portions.   275-38

The Priest was an individual who had received inspiration from within. And, realizing that such an influence or force might be given to others in their search for *why* and *what* were their purposes in material life, he then sought out one who might foster such a study in materiality.   281-42

And so this great descent into the Nile Valley was under way. One cannot help but wonder what the native Egyptians were to think of this "great horde" coming upon them from the north.

Egypt

When Arart and his tribe of 900 came into Egypt they found an agrarian people, unprepared by their life style to give any effective resistance to the invasion.

These were then, when conquered, not a warlike people — one not prepared for defense or of a way of defending self. Weapons only used in agriculture and in building, and these presenting the only modes of defense by the peoples during that period. Those of transportation being by that of the wheel and of the ox, and the beasts that were trained as domestic for the service of agriculture and of building, see?   900-277

The tribal invaders presented quite another standard. They were prepared to do battle for possession of the Nile Delta.

The people coming in, or the hills people, using the ways of warfare in that of the sling, and of those projections as were fastened to beasts and turning beasts loose on the people, who were *trained* animals to destroy the foes or enemies of the invaders — and, as is later seen, there becomes much of this same training in the Egyptian hill country, in which animals — bulls, bear, and the leopard, and the hawk, are trained to give the warfare against peoples that would war to these groups.

The modes of transportation were the end of the lighter-than-air crafts, the floating of wood or timbers in rafts and forms of boats, and of beasts of burden, and of afoot — being the war channels, see? and modes of transportation. Little of carriages, or wagons, or slides, had then been introduced by the invaders.   900-277

Q-1. What was the date, as man knows time, of this battle?
A-1. Ten thousand and fifty-six [B.C.].   900-275

Q-2. What was the color of the native Egyptian race, to which the entity belonged?

A-2. Near to the color of what would be called the true Chinese in the present — though the physiognomy of the face was entirely different, see?   849-45

The native ruler of Egypt was one named Raai who, like Ra Ta, was a man of high principle pursuing a metaphysical understanding of Creative Energy. Rather than clash with the invaders and shedding blood, Raai made a great concession. He subjected himself and his kingdom to the foreigners from the northeast.

9

The entity then that one whom the people overran, and in the name Raai, and the entity was of those peoples who first brought to that land the study of the relationships of man to the Creative Energy, and attempted to *establish* this relation with the peoples in the gathering and in the calling of same together, and neglected to countenance those that called on the entity for the defense against the hordes that came in from the North country, in the name of Arart, and the entity fought *little* with the peoples, subjecting self rather than making bloodshed for the peoples of the land, and through the application of self in the period — while condemned by others, condemned by [his] own peoples for the time — the entity gained *most* in *all* its experiences through that period.   1734-3

Raai's concession must have been an agonizing decision. Such an act is very rare in the history of nations and therefore sets an estimable example and precedent.

His action was appreciated by the invaders. This ruler's spiritual studies, and his concession of a materially wealthy land, gave Arart and Ra Ta a foundation for implementing their own parallel ideals. Indeed, the principle manifested in Raai's action became the basis for the studies of Jesus, thousands of years later when, as the readings say, He took His initiation in Egypt.

Not in merely submission, but in that the *principle* as was given *by* the entity *during* that period became the basis for the studies of the Prince of Peace, and the establishing *of* those schools as began in the land by those that overran the land.   1734-3

At this point, the building of a new nation was at hand — a monumental challenge of tact, diplomacy, ingenuity and political coordination. To appreciate the job which now faced Arart and Ra Ta, we should review what had become a most complex situation.

Egypt, which had just undergone the invasion by Arart's people, was experiencing immigrations from many different lands. The world, in its changing cycle, was undergoing great upheavals. People everywhere were on the move, and whole cultures were experiencing sudden changes.

Entering the Nile Valley during this period were people from Mongolia, India, Persia, Arabia, Assyria, Greece — and, of course, the dying continent of Atlantis. All these groups, combined with the native Egyptians, made up a great heterogeneity of political affiliations, commercial interests, religious customs, and cultural patterns. Such a widely differentiated citizenry made for many divisions, and conflicts now and again arose. It also yielded great potential, however, and created an eclecticism of varied spiritual and material resources with which to build the nation, and from understandings which would last a millenium.

10

The native government had exercised an extreme form of dictatorial control. It was structured to deal with a fundamental problem of life at that time. This was an intricate problem with roots going back to the beginning of time, and it involved religious, moral, political, and biological aspects. The symptoms were most readily apparent in the bodies of many individuals. These bodies were quite different from ours today.

Do not, my children, confuse thine bodies of today with those attributes of same, with the conditions existent in the Temple Beautiful.

281-25

At this time, traces of what the readings term physical "entanglements" were still prevalent. These initially occurred at an early stage of man's evolution when free-willed souls entered the earth's plane projecting their own thought forms into materiality. Souls became housed or "encased" in physical forms, which are probably the prototypes of mythological creatures such as unicorns, centaurs, mermaids, and those composite beings which became the gods of dynastic Egypt.

. . . appendages, that man in the experience inherited through the pushing of spirit into matter to become materially expressive . . .   3333-1

The passage of individuals through the experiences in the Temple of Sacrifice was much as would be in the hospitalization, or a hospital of the present day — when there have become antagonistic conditions within the physical body, such as to produce tumors, wens, warts or such.

Magnify this into the disturbances which were indicated, or illustrated in conditions where there was the body or figure of the horse, or the head of the horse with the body of man; or where there were the various conditions indicated in the expressions by the pushing of spirit into physical matter until it became influenced by or subject to same. Such influences we see in the present manifested as habits, or the habit-forming conditions.

281-44

These may be seen in a different manner presented in many of the various sphinxes, as called, in other portions of the land — as the lion with the man, the various forms of wing, or characterizations in their various developments. These were as presentations of those projections that had been handed down in their various developments of that which becomes man — as in the present.   5748-6

These, especially at that time were exhibited as feathers on the limbs of the native Egyptians . . .   585-12

These "forms" had entered the Nile Valley during the earliest period described in the readings (10,500,000 B.C.).

In those periods when the first change had come in the position of the land, there had been an egress of peoples — or *things*, as would be called today — from the Atlantean land, when the Nile (or Nole, then) emptied into what is now the Atlantic Ocean, on the Congo end of the country.

5748-6

In Atlantis, those who exhibited the most severe forms of these grotesque protuberances and appendages had been used as slaves for centuries.

The native Egyptians sought correction of this delicate racial question by way of absolute state control over mating and propagation. They regarded this as divine activity — not to be left to individual liberty. It was, in short, a program of selective breeding.

In the building, then, of the marital relationships that existed, these, as we understand, were not much as homes (as seen or understood as individual homes in the present). Rather were there the *appointed* companionships that were to serve their State, their purposes, for the completing of — or competing of — groups or nations one against another, and were rather the matter of the word of the ruler than that of choice of individuals, as known in the present.   294-149

The native Temple was the hub of State control, containing great halls of recreation and education, as well as chambers for birth and conception. There was no differentiation between "Church" and "State," or sacred and secular.

... for in this particular peoples all births were in this particular hall — or those set aside for same, as were those chambers in which conception was to have taken place, or to take place, for all the various relationships that existed among the peoples ...   294-149

This made for an unusual society. Homes and cities, as we know them today, did not exist.

As was seen, the housing of all the female of the whole clan or tribe for the evenings was in the temple, while those of the male that were outside those of the king's *own* household — and this included the king's alone — not any favorite or queen, or closer relationship, for all were in the same building, for they were under State rules. These were in tiers, as we would term today, beautifully laid out — with their halls, that were three and four tiers. The rooms, as would be sized as we would call, were 7 x 9 in their size, with 8 to 10 feet in the height, with those accoutrements for same — their rugs, their blankets, those that were wrought with the hands that made for the couches, for the various activities. Those that were born in same were immediately, or after three months, taken from their own families and raised in those groups which were confined in other buildings for those purposes. The great chambers or halls that were inter-between were of high tiers, that made for large halls, with the various forms of recreation — as the dance, etc ...   294-149

The ideals and endeavors in the "religious" practices were centered on a worship of the body — not in fulfillment of lusts, but in an attempt to acquire a more symmetrically beautiful body, a more perfect "temple for the living God."

> . . . for the physical attributes were worshiped much more in many ways in this period than the religious are in the present period, and rightly so . . .   294-148

Now that this government was yielding to invading tribal peoples, the natives would have to abandon their religious and social patterns.

The Atlanteans, who would enter from the West as Sons of the Law of One, had been dealing with the Law of One and spiritual, psychic abilities as part of their tradition for centuries. They had their own ideas as to how things should proceed.

These were the conditions which faced Arart and Ra Ta. It was their task to draw all this together coherently.

Chapter Two

THE NEW NATION

Politics

By mandate of conquest, Arart was now the ruler in Egypt, and it was initially understood that Ra Ta was the religious leader.

With Arart as the king and Ra Ta as the prophet or seer, there began a period that may well be called a division of interests of the peoples. Ra Ta attempted to induce the king to have only those natives that were tried and true in their acceptance of those attempts that would bring the closer relationship, according to those visions and experiences of Ra Ta in line with those being established as customs, rules and regulations.   294-148

With the entering of the group, or of this clan, little or no resistance was made by the natives as to the establishing of order until there began to be set up the laws as to what was the contribution or tax on peoples in the native land. And some native, and natives, raised questions — which made for first the political positions of groups in the land.   275-38

It quickly became apparent that compromise was necessary for peaceful settlement.

These conditions naturally made for some disturbance among the natives, that would be called the upper class, or those that sought to be in power themselves, or had ideas as to what should be done with the abilities of the peoples as individuals, and the abilities of the country as a country to supply those material necessities for sustenance and for recreation of the peoples.   294-148

Government roles had to be clearly delineated and powers balanced. The native Egyptians, or Uranians (as the readings say they were called), were allowed to share in the planning of a new state. This was one of Arart's initial acts of forbearance.

[165] acted as the keynote, or offering the first unselfish act for all those concerned, even when troublesome times arose by the activities of

14

the peoples subdued by the entity coming into the country, and by the development of the correlating of ideas of the wise men of [165's] court and of the then Urian [?] court, or Egyptian court.   165-5

Arart's most significant concession, perhaps following the precedent of Raai, was to abdicate the throne. He established a coalition government, naming his son, Araaraart, as King. Araaraart *shared* the rule with a native leader, who was given the family name — Aarat.

This eventually led to the pitting of the young leader with the king's son, and the change — or the accepting by the king of this native leader that represented a *group* as well as himself, for he was among those who had been native rulers and were deposed by the ruler whom Arart had found in office when settling there.   294-148

. . . and this ruler, Araaraart, being the second of the Northern Kings, and followed the rule of the father Arart, and began the rule, or took the position as leader, in his sixteenth year . . .   341-9

These pitted, then, as to their abilities to give to the peoples the better understanding of the mystic or mysterious forces as were made, and as *are* made, manifest in, then and now called, nature or natural forces.

254-42

Aarat had previously been the chief scribe, teacher, and sage of the native Egyptians.

Q-5. [900] as Aarat.
A-5. This entity we find the scribe in the temple, to whom the younger priests went for their instruction in the ways as were set by the peoples of the time. During this age we find that [900], or Aarat, was the sage of the cult of the true Uranians [?] or the peoples of the north hills.   341-9

Aarat's talents were aptly used in establishing the new order. For in contrast to the native state, and under the guidance of Ra Ta's vision, there was to emerge a system allowing freedom of decision and general equality. Aarat formulated these ideals into tenets.

In this capacity, then, we find the entity, Aarat, coming as the interpreter for the King [341], and for the Priest [294] (or chosen priest), by the tenets as were given, and as becoming acceptable to the peoples, and from same which was the first of records from which all of the thought and study of the worlds became — or to term in a different sense, the entity occupied the position of a Jefferson to the Declaration of Independence to the peoples in the religion and in the civil sense, see?   900-275

These tenets, which could be called the Declaration of Equality, contained the following:

An equal footing, equal consideration before the moral law, the penal law, the spiritual law.
Equal consideration for the material living experiences.

15

Equal opportunity for advancement owing to the individual development; the use of self as a servant to all.   341-44

The tenets were based upon definite spiritual precepts:

... we find in the rule of the second pharaohs in Egypt, when the laws were being given to the people in the understanding of the relations of the human mind, or soul, as to the heavenly or higher forces, the seeking after the temple not made with hands. The entity then was in that name of Aarat.   900-38

Ra Ta acted as High Priest to the nation, although it was not taken for granted that he should have this position.

The choosing of the leader [294] in the one set as Priest, this became a momentous question — as to who should be chosen. And when this was first set up, there arose many dissensions ...   254-42

In describing this government, one reading spoke in terms very familiar to Americans today.

... the entity was in the Egyptian land when there had been the setting up of an ideal by the Priest and especially by the King who had chosen the councilors for providing a better understanding between peoples of other lands and setting, as would be called in the present, the offices for the aid — or the Cabinet of — the President. Then the entity was President of the young King, as set by the choice of those in that period ...
The entity then was in the name of Henk-elel.   5395-1

Thus, peace and stability were gained, at least temporarily, within this complex of political and cultural conditions.
Araaraart's challenge was to pull the energies of the nation together for the activities necessary for material sustenance.
In the accomplishments then, we have as these in Araaraart. This: Much of the sealing of the peoples' abilities in being drawn together for the benefits of the masses rather than the classes ...   341-9

With this giving in (we are speaking of the political phase now) of the king to pit or parallel activities of the native with the abilities of the son, or heir, and he himself — the king — acting *as* a council then *with* Ra Ta to the inner council, there were the necessities of matching the abilities of the king's council, or king's people, with the facilities of the natives — as it were — in the various phases of what would be termed in the present as progress.   294-148

Advisory councils were established, and the functions of state were organized into departments.

In the choosing of the ones to lead, such councilors were chosen among the peoples of the land — both native and of those brought in.   254-42

With the political situation, then, the King — the young king, then only thirty — gathered about him many that were to act in the capacity of council, a portion [of] the inner council that ruled on the general circumstances of the peoples as a whole, then the council that had supervision over various parts or departments of the activities of the peoples, as would be termed in one's present surroundings as holding the various offices as a cabinet, the departments being much in that day as they are in the present . . . 294-148

. . . the entity was in the Egyptian land, during those periods when there were those activities setting up the various groups.

The entity was among the judges, or as was called – the advisory council to the King . . .

The entity was among the twelve councilors, then, during that period of activity. 289-9

With the appointing of such a body, to be sure there was much work for Ra Ta in council that there be kept the ideal or purpose for which this band, this group, had chosen this particular land for the development or manifestation of the forces that were manifesting through the mental or the spiritual man Ra Ta. 294-148

Commerce and Industry

A great industrialism began, at a level of technology undreamed of by academic historians. This included:

Mining:

Hence the opening by Araaraart of mines in Ophir, in what was later known as Kadesh, or in the land now called Persia. Also in the land now known as Abyssinia, and those portions yet undiscovered or used in the upper lands of the river Nile, there were those mines of the precious stones – as onyx, beryl, sardis, diamond, amethyst, opal, and the pearls that came from the sea near what is now called Madagascar. In the northern (or then the southern) land of Egypt, those mines that produced quantities – and quantities – and quantities – of gold, silver, iron, lead, zinc, copper, tin, and the like, that these might be matched with those in the valleys of the upper Nile. Also there was the producing of the stone-cutters who began gathering materials for the establishing of the residences of the incoming or the king's peoples. 294-148

. . . in the line of the exploration of the gases as were found in the hills below this land did the entity give much to the peoples. 1735-2

Granaries and storehouses:

There were also established storehouses, that would be called banks in the present, or places of exchange, that there might be the communications with individuals in varied lands . . . 294-148

Domestication of animals:

The entity's activities in the sojourn had to do with the domestication and use of the wild animal life and also those that later became the servants

17

with and of man in his activity; and brought about much that had to do with the raising of the horse from the smaller or pygmy animal to the charging steed; that had to do with the using of the wolves and the wild things for the closer companionship to man. 276-6

And some form of electricity was used:

And the entity was especially endowed with those abilities to draw from stones, from the clouds, from the elements, an influence that would *quicken* the activity of nature in its application to man; or what we call electrical forces in the present. 699-1

Talents were channeled by a division of labor, and the various trades developed.

Hence there became singers, workers in linen, workers in embroidery, carders, weavers, workers in clay, those in the various forms of commercial industry, those in horticulture, those in agriculture, and the various fields; for no merchants then existed, as there was one common store for all.
294-149

Architecture and engineering:

The entity then acted in the capacity to the king who *builded* those temples that spread to that *now* known as the pyramids, rather the obelisk [?], and those of the various standards in columns. 322-2

The entity [was] among those who prepared those edifices during that period, in plan, and in the way for the builders to do the actual work.
419-1

. . . for the entity began then to make for dwellings from without the caves and the preparation of same into those periods when not only stones were being used but also the preparation of the timbers, the preparation of other materials that were to be combined in the preparations for dwelling places. 870-1

Travel:

Q-1. What was the mode of transportation during this period in Egypt?
A-1. In this period there was the caravan, a portion of the lost forces as were seen in the lighter than air, and the forces of the force, as given, propelling in water. 953-24

With the economy functioning smoothly, and the government firmly established, communication began with other lands, facilitated apparently, by a common language throughout most regions.

. . . for even in this period (though much had been lost even by these peoples) was there the exchange of ideas with other lands, as of the Poseidian and Og, as well as the Pyrenean and Sicilian, and those that would now be known as Norway, China, India, Peru and American. These were not their names in that particular period, but from whence there were being gathered a portion of the recreations of the peoples; for the understandings were of one tongue! There had not been as yet the divisions

18

of tongues in *this* particular land. This was yet only in the Atlantean or Poseidian land. 294-148

Archaeology

While Araaraart organized the political, social and economic conditions, Ra Ta was formulating the spiritual principles of this emerging culture. He gathered together those who would take seriously a quest for higher knowledge. In the beginning these were few because the natives were skeptical.

It was through important archaeological discoveries that Ra Ta's word was given greater credence.

With the peaceful arrangements that were brought about, then, after the period of dissension with the young natives and the changing of the native's name to that of the king, Aarat, then the Priest was in the position of gradually gathering those that would harken to those words as pertaining to there being any relations with an outside world, or of there being those divisions in the body that were represented by those divisions of the intermission, or the body *of* intermission of an entity, from an experience to an experience. The natives held more strongly to the necessity of materialization for the enjoyment, as may be surmised from the conditions that were surrounded and evidenced in those particular conditions of this period.

With Ra Ta then beginning with the natives and those that listened to the uncovering of the records (in what would be termed archaeological research in the present), gradually more and more adherence was made to those words of this peculiar leader that had come into this land leading or guiding the conquerors, who were seeking for the expression of various thoughts that were coming through in those entities entering that group in that particular period. 294-147

And the entity was among those that counseled, being then the companion of one of the counselors that made for the search through the archaeological experiences in which the entities began to make the search for the older periods of the activities in the land. 695-1

The unearthing of the various tablets, various conditions, or as would be termed archaeology, was to the people of that period as much of a science as it is today — 1926, see? 900-277

. . . and the entity made for the building up of those influences for the archaeological researches as would be called of that day, as well as the preparations of stones, of gold, of all the various forms of building materials. 1265-1

The archaeological discoveries of that day played an important part in correlating and verifying the truths which Ra Ta wanted to implement.

19

. . . and with the unearthing of the tribal rites and ceremonies, the coalition of these truths we find were correlated with these peoples as were gathered about this ruler, and much of the architectural forces were set in motion. 341-9

.. for as these findings began to show the variations that had existed in the developing of the mental and physical needs of those peoples that had populated the land, these brought the changes in the manner in which those that had come, as well as natives, in the *way* in which these forces *were to* be expressed in this particular experience. 294-147

There were individuals who were educated in the deciphering of the texts being unearthed. Even in that day, "Egyptologists" had a place.

Q-13. [1100] as Aidol, afterwards Isisao, Scribe to High Priest.
A-13. This entity we find coming in favor with the King, being brought in from among the hills, where the unearthing of old monuments, and the entity then highly educated in the reading of the old inscriptions, hence coming in favor with all, giving the assistance to the King in creating the goodwill between the old and new inhabitants of the country. 341-9

What were the important discoveries that these early archaeologists made? The readings elaborate on this, referring to those early events in the Nile Valley mentioned in the prologue.

In this particular period of Araaraart and of the Priest . . . there was even then the seeking through those channels that are today called archaeological research.

In those periods when the first change had come in the position of the land, there had been an egress of peoples — or *things,* as would be called today — from the Atlantean land, when the Nile (or Nole, then) emptied into what is now the Atlantic Ocean, on the Congo end of the country.

What is now the Sahara was a fertile land, a city that was builded in the edge of the land, a city of those that worshipped the sun . . . The beginnings of these mounds were as an interpretation of that which was crustating in the land. (See, most of the people had tails then!) In those beginnings these were left.

When there was the entrance of Arart and Araaraart, they begin to build upon those mounds which were discovered through research.

5748-6

Apparently, Ra Ta, Arart, and Araaraart were uncovering — in 10,500 B.C. — the genesis of Egyptian culture, that evidence of the primeval convention which took place over ten million years ago, when *The Book of the Dead* was first conceived.

The entity then that one who became the recluse and hermit in the halls of the house of worship, learning the peoples first of the *chant* for the dead; and *The Book of the Dead* were a portion of the entity's own inscribing. In the name Itasldhoia. 115-1

. . . and the entity aided, in the latter portion, in writing much that is now a portion of *The Book of the Dead.* 454-2

The entity was then among those who came in from that now known as the Assyrian country, and brought many that became leaders in that builded up by the People when there was the return to the study of the relationships of individuals *to* individuals, and of individuals' relationship to the whole or to the Creative Energy. *Much* of that as was compiled by the entity became the ritual in that later known as *The Book of the Dead,* as well as of those who — in the lower portions of that land — later separated themselves and became a separate kingdom. 1924-1

At that time *The Book of the Dead* was known as the Book of Life. The following reading discusses its purpose:

. . . and the entity would do well to study even *The Book of the Dead,* as it was called in the present — yet in that experience it was rather the Book of Life; or it represents that which is the experience of a soul in its sojourn not only in the land of Nirvana [?], the land of Nod, or the land of night, but rather those things that make for the cleansing of a physical body for the aptitudes of expression through the senses or the emotions in the physical forces to the spiritual truths. 706-1

Social Reform

With verification from a much earlier era to encourage him, Ra Ta began injecting his visionary ideas into the religious and social establishments. He sought forms that would manifest a closer, organic harmony with the Creative Forces.

Seeing that propagation should be an act of spiritual consecration through free choice, he began to institute homes, replacing the system where companions were chosen by the state:

This particular relationship did the priest, or Ra Ta, attempt to change, in that there should be rather the establishing of the definite homes, as were in other lands that had been then visited by this priest, or from any; that these should be rather those of consecrated lives one to another. 294-147

These homes were to be based on that ideal of marriage where a man and woman live consecrated lives together and rear their own children, rather than releasing them to the state.

The attempt of the State to become the chooser of such was one of the factors over which the entity Oelom rebelled — as did the Priest and many of the others, see? For, the Priest had attempted to present the active forces such that the choice was to be upon the basis that companionship was *not* of a *physical* nature alone but of the mental and spiritual! 849-45

The logical conclusion of such an ideal was that a consecrated marriage could take place only between *one* man and *one* woman. This became law.

Ra Ta himself held to this ideal, taking one named Asua as his wife.

Temples

In addition to establishing homes and marriage, Ra Ta also began new forms of temple service. Initially, the native temple, which had been the center of State control, was used. The forms of service were changed, however.

> Hence there was the tendency of the changing or altering of those *forms* of service that were held in the temple . . .   294-149

Ra Ta gathered a small, tightly knit group together and began structuring the various aspects of spiritual service.

> Ra Ta began to gather his own people and those that were pointed out to him through the sources from which he received those various injunctions for the establishing of the name forever in the land. Hence, with these, there were the preparations for the temple where there were to be the various forms of worship, as related to the divisions of the penal or moral relationships of the peoples, and what would be termed or called in the present the religious or spiritual relationships.   294-148

> In the one before this we find in the land where the peoples were first given the laws as led to the separation of the peoples from the worships of *physical* beings.   2484-1

Soon Ra Ta's visions began to take concrete form in the construction of buildings to be known as the Temple Beautiful and the Temple of Sacrifice.

> With the gathering of these people and places, there began the erecting of the edifices that were to house not only the peoples, but the temple of sacrifice, the temple of beauty — that *glorified* the activities of individuals, groups or masses, who had *cleansed* themselves for service.   294-148

> The Temple of Sacrifice was a physical experience, while the Temple Beautiful was rather of the mental — in which there was the spiritualization — not idolizing, but crystallizing of activities or services to a special purpose — or specializing in preparation for given offices of activity.
> 281-43

With the physical cleansings that took place in the temple services, many persons

> . . . gradually lost, then, many feathers from their legs. Many of them lost the hairs from the body, that were gradually taken away. Many

gradually began to lose their tails, or their protuberances in their various forms. Many of them gradually lost those forms of the hand and foot, as they were changed from claws — or paws — to those that might be more symmetrical with the body. Hence the activities or the uses of the body, as they became more erect and more active, more shaped to them in their various activities.   294-149

The passage of individuals (to be sure, by choice) through the experiences in the Temple of Sacrifice was much as would be in the hospitalization, or a hospital of the present day . . .   281-44

In the Temple of Sacrifice there is the falling away of those influences in which man had come by his projection of self into matter that there might be the satisfying of desires of flesh as in animal associations and matter relating one to another; which feeding upon itself, as flesh upon flesh, bringeth corruption in the very souls of men. So was there the breathing upon the bodies that there might be the crucifying of the activities in the desires of body, the desires of flesh, the crucifying of those desires as in relation one to another. These must be blotted out as each soul offers itself in sacrifice that it may be put upon the altars or fires of love and *burned*, as it were, that there might be that purification in the flesh, that there might become again the dross burned away and the pure soul be one with that Creative Energy.   275-43

For, in the period, there was the Temple of Sacrifice; or that wherein the body was shed of the animal representations through the sacrificing of the desires of the appetite, through the *changing* of self in the temple service.   275-33

The readings give this description of the altars in the Temple of Sacrifice:

And upon the altar would be only the fire, not a sacrifice . . . The altar should be of stone, or stone in color; not wholly symmetrical in the sizes of the stones, for some would be round, some oval, some nearly square. But the top would be indicated as being flat. The fire, of course, would be indicated as of twelve sticks — by fire on same; this indicating the twelve centers of the body to be purified.   585-10*

The readings elaborate on the structure of the Temple Beautiful, showing that its name was very appropriate:

In structure, this: There had been gathered from all the nations of the earth that which represented from their environ, their surrounding, the most beautiful gift; that it might be a reminder of those, to those, that purified or gave themselves in service or activity there, of the beauty of service of *every* land in this preparation of the bodies for their greater service and for their intermingling with those of the earth's environ as well as enabling the servants, the workers, the priestess, the prophetess, those that labored — or joyously gave themselves — to give their activity for others.

*Description for a life seal.

23

The materials outwardly were of the mountains nigh unto the upper waters of the Nile.

It was in the form of the pyramid, within which was the globe — which represented to those who served there a service to the world.

The furnishings may be surmised from the fact that the most beautiful things from each land were gathered there: gold, silver, onyx, iron, brass, silk, satins, linen.   281-25

An affirmation appeared over the entrance to the Temple Beautiful:

... that as written over the door of the Temple Beautiful: *PARCOI SO SUNO CUM* [?]. LORD, LEAD THOU THE WAY. I COMMIT MY BODY, MY MIND, TO BE ONE WITH THEE.   281-25

On the right side of the altar (and these should be balanced) would be depicted in the distance the Temple of Beauty, or Temple Beautiful. This would be indicated by the seven pillars, with the star on the central pillar ...   585-10*

The services conducted there were equally beautiful and inspiring:

As to the manner of the service there: The individuals having cleansed themselves of those appendages that hindered, came not merely for the symbolic understanding. For these, to be sure, were all symbolized — the faults, the virtues of man, in all his seven stages of development — in the light or the lamp borne by those who served as the Light Bearers to those who entered for their initiation, or for their preparation to be that as given by the teachers — even *Ra Ta.*

Laying aside those things that easily beset the sons of men, ye as ye enter here, put thy whole trust in the one God, that ye may be all things unto all men, thereby crucifying thine own desires that they — thy brethren — may know the Lord their God.   281-25

Worship included music and chanting:

Turn for the moment, then, to thy service in the Temple Beautiful. Here we have those incantations that are as but the glorifying of constructive forces in all of their activity within the human emotions that may be known in the present day; for glory, not of self, not of the ability of self, but the glory of the oneness of purpose, of the I AM of the individual for the glorifying of that creative energy within self that may keep the whole body, whole body-individual, whole body as of the group, the whole body as of those within the sound as it ranges from the highest to the lowest of the incantations within; following that known in thine own present as i-e-o-u-e-i-o-umh ... the intoning in of self within; that there might come, as it were, the sound as of many waters; or as the morning stars in their circuit about the earth may sing with the glorious coming of the light into the experience of man to raise same to his at-oneness and his attunement with those beauties of the coming of the sons of men into the earth that God in His Oneness of Purpose may bring those activities with the sons of

*Description for a life seal.

24

God as an at-onement in *their* purposes in the earth. The glorifying of Him in the dealings and associations with the fellow man, and these find their attunement in each chord as it rings one with another in all the music that may be heard from every sound that follows in eeiu-u-u-ummmm in its *forms,* through that attunement along the pineal to the source of light within the self to make for the emotions of glorifying alone.   275-43

In the activities then, there were first the songs, the music, as we have indicated that *ye* sing: Ar-r-r — Ou-u — Ur-r; which makes for the losing of even the association of the body with that save the *vibrations* of which the body was then composed; yea now is, though encased in a much more hardened matter, as to materiality; which made for the vibrating of same with light, that *becomes* color, that becomes tone, that becomes activity.

281-25

And dance:

The entity then was among those that were raised to high position in that of the dancer, or entertainer in the temple . . .   454-2

There were symbolic rituals portraying the stages of spiritual growth and the mysteries of life:

Then there was the giving by the Prophetess of the seal of life that was set upon each and every one who passed through these experiences, how or in what field of activity the relationships were of an individual to its fellow man in maintaining material existence; being in the world yet not *of* the world.

These then, made for that as ye have in thine experiences in the present expressed: First in cleanliness, in purifying of the body, in the washing in blood, in water, that ye may be purified before thyself first and then before others. The anointing with the incense, making for the raising of that ye know as thine senses or perception or consciousness of the activities to all the faults, by comparison, as arose among others . . .

In the latter portion, when there had been those cleansings of the feet in thy own service there, then the activities were in the Temple Beautiful: as a Guard to those as they proceeded from one symbol to another in their journey about the Temple . . .

Q-3. [585]: *What part did I take in services in the Temple Beautiful?*
A-3. The Announcer with the cymbal and horn.

Q-4. [5773]: *Please give me the information as to whether or not I was in the Temple Beautiful. If so, please give that service which I rendered.*
A-4. An observer of those seals wherein the effects of the sojourns in the varied activities were to be seen, or the effects from the planetary sojourn. Hence a *keeper* of seals there.

Interest in astrology, astronomy, arises from same.

Q-5. [603]: *Was I in the Temple Beautiful and what part did I take in the services?*
A-5. In the station where thy weakness now appears. Take this home with thee and find what thou must do!

A giving of the station, the symbol in that stage where the birth of the entity, the soul, was from materiality into materiality, or the mystic forces as considered of how thought or mind in its flow makes for associations of ideas as to make for the conscious consciousness of the entity . . .

Q-7. [5774]:
A-7. In the records of that given for each in the journey *out* of the Temple to material application. Or, to put in the parlance of today, a secretary to the stations.   281-25

In explaining this "journey" through the Temple Beautiful, the readings indicate that it was a very large place.

Here it may be well that there be given a concept of what is meant by the journey, or what journey is meant. As indicated, it, the globe within the pyramid without, was four forty and four cubits (twenty-seven and one-half inches was a cubit then, or a mir [?] then). The height was four and twenty and forty and four mir [?], making then that in the form of the ova, or the egg in its ovate form.

From station to station in the seven phases or seals or stands or places of the activities, they were such as to make each station lead from one to another by ever crossing the one; making the continued web.   281-25

The readings show that two orders of priesthood were in charge at the temples. Each carried out specific functions:

Q-18. Were sacrifices offered by the High Priest, Ra Ta?
A-18. No. Sacrifice offered by the Sacrificial Priests, High Priests being those who waited on the peoples, only offering the emblematical for the King and King's favorites. We find the same in that later given in the Wilderness, when Aaron [was] made High Priest. The High Priest only offering that as prepared by sacrificial priests at certain periods.   341-10

Q-9. [294] as High Priest.
A-9. In the name of Ra Ta and was the Priest who gave the entrance into the Holy of Holies to the King and then gave the rule to the people, falling in disfavor and banished by the King.   341-9

The readings suggest that the Temples of Beauty and Sacrifice were located at what is now Giza, but was then the Holy City called Aicerao:

The entity was then among those who . . . [came] to the temples about that place now where the various forms of the figures present, or represent, the attempts of the peoples in the day, and about those yet to be uncovered, in the city *then* called Aicerao.   358-3

Besides the native temple and the Temples of Beauty and Sacrifice which were still in preparatory stages, there was yet another temple in the area referred to as Luz. This was the Temple of the Sun, and it performed quite another function.

26

Q-2. Mr. [599], as Sisod.

A-2. In this same rule, in the capacity of executioner to the Keeper of the Sun Temple, where the ones were kept who were to be executed or banished.   341-10

Later, as the Egyptian culture developed, there would come two other temples — the Temple of Initiation, and the Temple of Records.

Travel

Although Ra Ta was very busy establishing Temple life, he found it necessary to spend time traveling, gaining knowledge from other regions.

Hence we find the activities of the priest, or seer, as really a busy life — yet much time was given in keeping self in communion with those that brought the knowledge of that progress made in the spiritual sense in other lands, especially so from Poseidia and Og.   294-148

But Ra Ta went to Atlantis for more than studying teachings of the Law of One. Atlanteans were now beginning to enter Egypt, and there were negotiations involving the records of Atlantean history. The Sons of the Law of One knew their continent would soon be destroyed, and it was decided that a copy of their records should be stored in Egypt.

. . . at this time there was the coming into the land the Atlantean peoples. These were going back and forth, for the periods of the rebellious influences, the activities of varied individuals in the Atlantean land were active in this period . . . and Egypt was chosen as one of those places where the records of that activity or peoples were to be established.   275-38

Through these activities Ra Ta met and joined forces with one of the most important Atlanteans of that time, Hept-Supht, the Atlantean patriarch in charge of the Records.

For, the entity was still in charge of these records when the last of the peoples of Atlantis journeyed to the various quarters of the globe; but Alta, Zeus, Zephyrus, and the recorder of Alta were friends, associates — yea, descendants in the flesh with and of the same as the entity . . .

And, as there was the entering of the Priest from the land Egypt to Poseidia, that there might be gained more of an understanding of the Law of One (or God), that there might be the interpretations and the records of same carried to the Egyptian land, the *entity* returned — or *journeyed,* soon after the Priest's return from Atlantis, to Egypt.

Hence, as there continued to be the rebellions and the exodus of the peoples in Atlantis before the final destruction, the entity — becoming interested in those activities — finally (as would be termed in the present) became embroiled through engrossment in that taking place in Egypt during the young king's enthronement — and the elderly king, and the peoples, and the counselors of the king.

And when there was the pitting of the young King against the royal native Aarat, the entity then took counsel — as it were — with self, and made Egypt the home.   378-13

He, with the modern ideas among a peoples that were attempting to adjust themselves to the varying conditions, joined with the Priest in bringing something of order in the laws and in the direction of conditions in the period.   275-38

Hept-Supht was an imposing figure and a powerful asset to Ra Ta in his enterprise.

The Atlantean [378] five feet ten inches, weighing a hundred and sixty pounds; color as of *gold* that is burnished; yet keen of eye, gray in color. Hair as golden as the body. In activity alert, keen, piercing in vision, and of influence on those that approached.   275-38

Q-1. Give in detail the psychic powers he developed at that time.
A-1. This would almost be impossible. To put such into words would be as impractical as it would be to describe what the multiple of colors as related to vibrations brings, reduced to its eleventh or nth degree.   378-13

While Ra Ta was away on these foreign travels, dissension and backsliding, that went so far as sensual indulgence, were increasing at home.

In these visitations that were caused, or that necessitated the absenting of the Priest from these places, there arose more and more a dissension with those peoples that there was being builded much that was being left to subordinates, as considered by some of the native councilors — and a few also of those that allowed avarice to arise in their own make-up. This brought questioning more and more, and there began to be the use of those things that gradually turned the minds of those associated in the offices that had been set aside by the Priest in their activity, in the use of, in the brewing and concocting of drinks that set the body, set the mind, set the whole fires of physical body against that as had been cleansed by the fires on the altars, as were in the sacrificial temples.   294-148

When Ra Ta returned from an archaeological dig, he found these activities desecrating the Temple of Sacrifice, and "there arose a mighty turmoil."

In the third series, or — as they were set aside as periods of ten years, most of those buildings were completed, and when there was the return of Ra Ta from one of these visits to the mount — where there had been some activities on the part of those that were delving into what was termed the archaeological conditions of those that had lived in the lands in the periods before — and there was found in the Temple of Sacrifice the aggrandizing of the lusts of the body, rather than those activities that were to be carried on by the sacrificial priests — there arose a mighty turmoil . . .   294-148

We can imagine the anger, shame, guilt and resentment that such a development caused. A conspiracy against Ra Ta grew from this incident.

> ... there were sought various ways and manners in which there might be fault found with the activities of those conditions that surrounded the body, and there arose at that time the first — as may be said — of that saying, "When the devil can't get a man any other way, he sends a woman for him."
>   294-148

Chapter Three

TIMES OF TRIAL

Banishment

> . . . and divisions arose that were even unknown then to Ra Ta, for he being among those that trusted all, believed all, and — as it were — for the time the gods laughed at his weakness!   294-148

Conspiracy always involves subtle intrigue, and when people join in duplicity the facts become elusive. It is difficult to understand exactly where or why Ra Ta went wrong, but powerful temptations were involved. The conspiracy was an attempt to trick Ra Ta into violating his own precepts, and thus cause him shame. Adam's temptation was Eve, and it was a woman who would unwittingly bait the trap for Ra Ta.

> Among those, then, of the priests' daughters, was one of the King's favorites — that made for the entertaining of the King and his council, and his visitors — who was more beautiful than the rest, and she was induced to gain the favor of the Priest through the activities of herself in body, and in the manners that would induce some fault to be found. This was not by her own volition, but rather by the counsel of those that made for the persecutions of her own peoples that were being protected by the activities of the body . . .   294-148

This did not please Araaraart; this woman, Isris, was:

> Daughter of the second priest in the rule, and gave of self in the service in the temple as the dancer before the King in temple service, and in high favor with the King.   341-9

An arrangement was apparently made for Isris to have closer contact with Ra Ta in the temple. They were an excellent physical match, Ra Ta being one of "unusual appearance" and Isris "being of beautiful figure and form." (538-9)

The readings imply a proposition made by the conspirators that

Ra Ta and Isris conceive a child, in order to produce a perfect human form.

> As these began then, with this favorite of the King — and the better of the forms that had become near the body beautiful, or beauty divine, those activities in the temple (not the Temple Beautiful, but in the temple) brought these individuals, as individuals, into closer relationships, and the decree eventually came that the Priest was to be, then, the companion of this body that had been chosen to be the channel through which those activities were to bring to those peoples a body such as the Priest had spoken of . . .   294-149

Evidently, Ra Ta was attracted to the idea of being progenitor of such a divine body, and the beauty of Isris may well have been an influence, for the Priest "fell for the whole proposition." (294-149)

Thus Ra Ta succumbed to the strategy — he had procreated by state decree and violated the law of monogamy. When the child was born the opposition was quick to step forward in condemnation, pointing out the obvious contradiction:

> . . . when there came — as it were — the offspring with this association, then there became the cry that there was the breaking of the very laws that had been set by the Priest, who was to make for the home and the changing of the conditions for the peoples, and more and more were the lines drawn as to the sides that were taken.   294-149

A heated debate ensued which brought about "many various divisions." (294-149) The issues pitted brother against brother:

> Here we find the entity was in very unusual relationships with the Priest, Ra Ta. For, the entity was the brother of the Priest in that experience, though in opposition to the activities of same when there were those influences that brought about the banishment of the Priest from the Egyptian land.
> For, the entity sided not only with some of the counselors to the King, but with the natives who rebelled at that period.   2345-1

And son against father, for Ra Ta's son, Ral-La-Ral, stayed

> . . . with the King rather than going even with the father; for he sided with the King as to the tenets that made for this rebellion, for the Priest making the law was to him the law, and broke the law; and the son, though in tender years, with the Council, rebelled.   282-7

Because the final judgment rested with the King (and also, perhaps, because Isris had been a favorite), there quickly developed "the first uprising between Church and State." (294-148)

> *Q-19. What did this High Priest do to cause disfavor in the eyes of the ruler?*
> A-19. It being permissible for the Priest to have only one wife, and this High Priest taking of the daughters of the second sacrificial priest and

a favorite to the King, as the Concubine to the Priest, this brought in the forces of rebellion . . .   341-10

The King had a momentous decision to make. The nation's spiritual leader was in obvious violation of the law and Araaraart had to choose the punishment to be meted out to the one who was the motivating force behind the Temples of Beauty and Sacrifice.

All activities ceased, and in the temples:

> . . . there were the incense burnings for those peoples that were amiss in their relationships of the alien and the native, of the priest gone astray, and the King bowed in sorrow, of the native in the hills, and of the shepherds waiting for news from those in power.   2686-1

There was one man who clearly understood penal law and what must follow: Asriaio, a native Egyptian who rose to the office of Chief Councilor.

> . . . the entity rises from among his own people to the position of Chief Councilor, during the reign of the first conqueror [165] of this people, but is retained as the counselor to that ruler. When the second ruler [341] rises to position, still retained as Chief Councilor . . .   953-24

It was Asriaio who convinced Araaraart that Ra Ta should be banished from Egypt.

> . . . and at the time of the divisions among the peoples, on account of conditions arising between the High Priest, or the head of the religious study [294], as would be termed today, the Councilor persuaded, ruled, as it were, with the King, for the banishment of the ruler priest, for, as is set, the law *above* that of the maker . . .   953-24

Finally:

> . . . there was the eventual trial of this Priest and the companion, and they were then banished into the land that lies to the south and east of this land, or the Nubian land* . . .
> In the land to which these were banished, not only were there the two — but a *number*; some two hundred and thirty-one souls.   294-149

Hept-Supht, the Atlantean leader, was among those banished with Ra Ta and Isris:

> And with this establishing came that period when the Priest [294] broke the law that was set by him concerning the number of wives accorded or given to the priest. And this brought first the political uprising. Then the religious war. And the Priest with the princess [538] was banished, with all those that adhered to the Priest's activity, including the aide to the Priest [Hept-Supht] to the Libyan land.   275-38

Rhaha, second in line in the order of High Priest, replaced Ra Ta as head of the priesthood of the nation.

*Also referred to in the readings as Libya and Abyssinia.

Q.-8. [228] as Rhaha.
A-8. The High Priest of the people in this same era that overshadows the peoples in the troubles that arise in the Holy Temples. The entity then became Priest to the King and head of the priesthood of the nation.　341-9

The children of the Priest, [282], [288], were left in the land of Egypt as political hostages, and religious hostages.　275-38

The imprisonment of Iso, the child of Ra Ta and Isris, caused considerable torment for not only those who were banished but also for the King. There was a lack of parental love among those in charge of keeping the Priest's children.

The entity then among those who were in the keeping of those as were banished by the King when divisions arose, keeping especially the young of those that were so banished. In the name then Asie, and the entity gained, and then lost mightily, in that as was attempted to be perpetrated — as it were — by the entity's position. Loving rather the suffering of those that were banished, and desiring to put self in an exalted position with those in power.　37-1

Because of these turmoils, this little girl died when only four years old.

Q.-11. [288] as Iso.
A-11. The offspring to the two as banished from the King, and only lived a short while in the banishment, only the presence to the King causing consternation in the camps where banishment was given to the hills and rivers.　341-9

Q-21. To what age did Iso live, and what was the connection of this body with the King? Was she banished with the parents?
A-21. This body, we see, in the fourth to fifth year. Not banished to hills. Kept by the King, as for the respect of the mother, the favorite, and kept in the House of the Sun, or in the Sun Temple under that rule, and this brought the constant consternation to the King, as to whether he was justifiable in banishment, or would not this have been better other ways. Listened, however, to the Councilor who sought this banishment.　341-10

The offspring, to be sure, was taken — as others — from this relationship, and in their various forms and manners there was the attempt to be brought about the proper conditions, yet it wasted away — for while there were the abilities of the Priest in some directions, yet these had not clarified or crystallized into that which came about in the latter part of this experience for the entity.　294-149

The child [288] fair of body, of hair — only four and a half when passing on, through sorrow of separation.　275-38

Asua, Ra Ta's lawful wife:

. . . lost faith in self and in those who made profession to lead others

toward that knowledge of the higher forces in earth through man's relation
to the Creator. 369-3

With the spiritual leader of the nation gone, a spirit of rebellion
took root.

Here all became changed, with this tumult that arose with the various
priests that were in attendance in the various offices, and advantage was
taken of the situation by many of those who in their various forms began
to *learn*, as it were, a form of war and defense, and there were the gathering then of the young men, the old men, and sides were taken. Still some
remained faithful to the priests who remained in the land, and troublesome
times arose for many, many suns, or until at least nine seasons had passed
before there was even the *semblance* of the beginning of a quieting, and
that not until there had been definite arrangements made that the Priest
would return and all would be submissive to his mandates; and he became,
then, as may be termed in the present, a dictator — or a monarch in his
own right. 294-149

Rebellion

. . . and advantage was taken of the situation by many of those who in
their various forms began to *learn*, as it were, a form of war and defense,
and there were the gathering then of the young men, the old men, and
sides were taken. 294-149

In addition to the many divisions in the wake of the Priest's
banishment, native resentments also flared up. Araaraart had to turn
from his anguish over Ra Ta, Isris and little Iso, to cope with forces
which threatened his throne. For a time, chaos destroyed all constructive movement in Egypt.

The first danger came within the King's own household — from
his brother, Ralij.

. . . the brother of the ruler who gave the first laws to the peoples of
the indwelling of the Higher Forces as might be manifest in the earth's
plane. The entity then in the name of Ralij, and was first the hindrance to
the brother . . . 78-1

Ralij had been given charge over a principality named the Ibex,
which was supposed to pay fealty to Araaraart's administration in
Luz. However, difference in principle between the religious leaders
of Ibex and Luz began to develop, and those in Ibex seemed to
favor a policy of self-interest:

The entity then was among those who were in the Ibex Rebellion,
being among those of the household of the young King's brother; keeping
the tenets of those who expressed in that activity: "If you don't take care
of yourself, no one else will do it for you."

34

This isn't true. If you live right yourself, everyone will take care of you.

3479-2

A soothsayer named Udarr took particular issue with Ra Ta, and contributed to the Priest's banishment. Udarr was active in the religious activities of the Ibex:

> There again the entity was a soothsayer; one who reckoned by the aspects of the sea — its sand, and the tides, and the sun and the shadows.
>
> There the entity partook of those things that were oft in conflict with those that were set up by that entity who was the Priest of the day.
>
> Hence there the entity, with some of those counselors, wrought much that caused the banishment of the Priest; during those periods when there were the activities in which the Priest as an entity gave material manifestations in affections which were used by *this* entity, Udarr, as the cause for the bringing about of turmoils, when the real reason was because of the variations in principle of that taught by this entity and that taught by the Priest.
>
> Then the entity again was active in setting the signs, the marks upon those places in Ibex, and in those places later known as Heliopolis, that caused many to be led astray; for they bound rather than loosed in truth.

1580-1

The readings suggest that a major issue in these differences was the question of animal worship — certainly a dangerous focus of spiritual energy at a time when many sought to be free of "animal appendages." Because the leaders of the Ibex were relatives of Araaraart and Ra Ta, animal worship must have been imported from that tribe's place of origin.

> Then in the name Valtui, the entity was in the associations of the King's or leader's household; then among the associations in the land that made for activities in the Arabian land that brought into Egypt that which made animal worship in a portion of the people's activities much later; not by the entity's actions but an associate of the entity.   276-6

We are told of Ra Ta's son Ral-La-Ral:

> In the leading of the people to the services of those before the beasts, the entity failed, for this brought in those of another people that led the peoples later astray. There the Ibex *with* the entity again locked horns.

282-2

And one of Ra Ta's daughters, Ar-Ela, was in "close associations through the experience with leaders of the rebellions."

> Then the entity was in the name El (meaning beautiful) — Ar-Ela. In the experience the entity was held almost in as much reverence as the companion of the Priest, [Isris, later named] Isis; and many of the figures of the entity were a part of the hieroglyphics that later became a part of the worshipfulness of many of the peoples. Because of the entity's close

associations with those who were the animal worshipers, these brought discouraging and disconcerting activities, but they eventually came to be channels through which great help came to the peoples in that experience.

1857-2

The intensity of this "cold war" between principalities increased after the banishment of Ra Ta. The Ibex began to side with those now in rebellion against Araaraart. The King's orders were ignored.

These differences of principle and the enmity between brothers broke into war after Ralij kidnapped some of the women of Araaraart's court. He then declared the Ibex a separate kingdom.

> The entity was then among those in the household, or in that city of Ibex in the period when there were the setting aside of many of the orders of the King and the taking up of those that had brought rebellion in the land, and the taking away of some of the favorites of the King.   457-2

> The entity was among the natives who rose in rebellion and made for those activities that allowed the opportunities for the Prince of Ibex to withdraw and make his own expressions of desertion to activities of the King and the Court.   1347-1

In the conflict, both sides were equipped with armies. One Ja-Ja-Guar was the leader of the rebellious forces:

> Before that the entity was in the Egyptian land, when there was the Ibex Rebellion – or when the household of the King rebelled. The entity then was in that position as the leader of the army, or the rebellious forces; and aided in setting up the activities in Ibex.   2809-1

And Is-Thk-El commanded Araaraart's army:

> It was during those periods when turmoils and strifes arose, when the Priest was being banished and when there were the uprisings of the natives as well as the rebellions in the house of the King himself.

> The *entity* then was among those who would be called today the leaders of the soldiery, or in command of the King's Guard during that experience.

> Thus the entity made for many friends and foes of those that were of the rebellion.   991-1

While Araaraart was involved in the Ibex confrontation there were others threatening to undermine his throne. Now, when the King's rule was weakest, the Atlanteans were arriving in force.

> Before that we find the entity was in that now known as the Atlantean or Egyptian land; for the entity was in both, being the one who conducted, as it were, those in authority of the Law of One to the Egyptian land for the sojournings of the peoples there, at the time of or just previous to the last destruction of the Atlantean land.

> The entity then was in the capacity of the director of the expedition ...   955-1

36

Although most of the Atlanteans were followers of the Law of One, their actions sometimes demonstrated that spiritual affiliation does not necessarily insure kindness and consideration.

In addition, some of the Sons of Belial covertly entered Egypt.

> Then the entity, in the name Sane-Naid, was beautiful in body; tempting many in these relationships at times, especially the Sons of Belial who crept in with those from the Atlantean land into Egypt. 989-2

When Ax-Tell, the leader of these powerful foreigners, arrived in Egypt he was not pleased with the situation.

> The entity came then, in the name Ax-Tell, from those forces that were in charge of the Law of the One.
>
> In establishing self in that land, the entity found little of help; finding fault with the king in power, finding little in common with the priest that led; finding those things that measured not to that standard the entity had had in the land, withdrew on account of the associations – specifically – of the priest with those women, or those of the opposite sex in the land. 487-17

If Ax-Tell did not find conditions in Egypt measuring up to his standard, many Atlanteans thought the same of the native Egyptians. These immigrants had brought with them many "things" or servants of man/animal composite form. The Atlanteans had specific attitudes concerning them. Ra Ta clearly disagreed with those attitudes.

The Atlanteans believed

> That all those who were without sufficient of the purposes to seek the whole light, because of the very influence of the appendages and conditions which had been manifested in materiality such as to make them "things," were to be kept submerged to be used by those with the greater abilities. The Priest held that these were one, and that such conditions offered the possibilities through which each soul might find a way of escape – by and through the purifying of the body in each experience, that the activities of same – in its passage through the various experiences necessary – might eventually become channels through which blessings, and knowledge of the divine influence and force, might be made manifest. 281-44

Many of the Atlanteans classified the natives as being hardly more advanced than their servants.

> For they had brought with them (as had the Priest) many *things,* or individuals, or entities, that were without purpose – or merely automatons, to labor or act for the leaders in the various spheres of activity.
>
> And, as the natives found, such beings were being classified or judged to be such as many of the natives of the land. 281-43

The native Egyptians were caught between two powerful forces, and were receiving most of the abuse. The King's Guard now held attitudes similar to the Atlanteans and were attempting to segregate and oppress the original inhabitants of Egypt.

> Then, we find the entity was in the Egyptian land when there were those disturbing factors owing to the activities and uprisings of the natives, the disturbing forces as created by the activities of the King when changes were made — or the pitting of one against the other of the natives that had arisen and cried for justice and mercy.   1438-1

The natives were not ready to tolerate such intimidation, and being classified as a "thing" brought considerable disquiet to one native, Oelom, who "was among those who would be called today the intelligentsia of the period." (849-45)

> Then, in those periods when there was the entering of the Atlanteans, with those *things* or servants, and the attempts of the leaders there to classify many of the natives with such groups as had been brought in by the King, the Priest and the Atlanteans, there came consternation in the experience of the entity Oelom.   849-45

Oelom joined with the rebellion in Ibex, not in agreement but as a means to an end, and he led a revolution against the throne.

> Thus, though not wholly in accord with the uprising or the conditions which had arisen by the rebellions in the house of the King himself, the entity joined in same, or rather used the same as a means, as an end to gain the purposes — as well as to prevent that classifying or segregation which was being attempted by portions of the King's Guard or King's Council.   849-45

> The entity then among those who rose in rebellion at the expulsion of the Priest, and led against that throne . . .   849-1

The purpose of Oelom's revolution was to force the return of Ra Ta.

> There we find the entity was among those closely associated with some in the Rebellion; being of the natives who rebelled, owing to the activities as brought about, and the needs for the consideration — even by the natives, and others — for the return of the Priest.
> The entity then was the companion of the native, or wife of that native who led the Rebellion — at the time of the Ibex Rebellion, as well as during the period of the entrance of the peoples from Atlantis.   2037-1

Oelom and the native leaders now felt that only Ra Ta could restore justice, being the only match for the powerful Atlanteans.

> When the Atlanteans in that experience began to influence the spiritual and moral life of the Egyptians, under those turmoils which had arisen through the Rebellions as indicated, there came that desire, that purpose — especially on the part of the natives, as well as those who had been adherents partly to the tenets of the Priest — that the Priest be returned, that there might be a better understanding. For the native leaders, espe-

cially, realized that their own activities or representation in the spiritual, moral and religious life would be destroyed if there was the adhering to the tenets being presented by the Atlanteans.

And, as might be termed in the present, some indicated that the Priest alone would be a match for those activities of some of the stronger or more forward Atlanteans.   281-43

As the Ibex and Oelom rebellions grew in intensity, it became dangerous to be undecided in the cross-fire of the various factions.

The entity was divided between those of the native rebellion and of the Ibex rebellion. And these brought those periods of unrest . . . for he had been imprisoned by those who doubted his abilities or his activities from both the Ibex groups and the King's and the natives'. And in the Temples of the Sun had the entity been incarcerated for those periods of nearly half the period of the Priest's exile.   1334-1

With the Oelom and Ibex rebellions to contend with, Araaraart faced yet a third threat to his position. The Atlanteans, taking advantage of the chaos, moved to usurp the King's power.

. . . the entity was among those who came into Egypt who were in authority in the Atlantean land; being among the children of the Law of One, and instrumental in influencing the peoples to the uprising – or to the attempt to take advantage of the situation when the Atlanteans came into Egypt . . .

For, then – as called by her peoples – the entity was a princess, or a daughter of a ruler of the peoples in Atlantis.

The name was Ax-El-En-Ta.   2487-1

Ax-El-En-Ta, with another Atlantean, It-El-Sut, sought to establish their leader, Ax-Tell, in authority.

And then with the entering of the Atlanteans, the entity was favored with the leader of the Atlanteans, especially as an effort to establish one of the leaders to some position of power; that brought the entity's associate almost into disrepute when there was the attempt to partially usurp the King's authority or power. This was Ax-Tell.   808-18

It is important to note, however, that not all Atlanteans favored this political move, the prejudice against the natives, or the slavery of the "things."

For instance, one Atlantean, Ajax-Ol, "did not favor the activities of the leader of the Atlanteans in the rebellion, it brought questionings of his peoples." (2462-2)

Another Atlantean, Assen-ni, was opposed to slavery and recognized hypocrisy among those of the Law of One.

And there was the realization by Assen-ni that those who had been born were through no fault of their own being used as creatures for exploitation . . .

As the entity saw then, and as it experiences in the present, the education is not to fit an individual to be lord or master but for service — better service; whether in the ministry to the needs of the material man, the mental man or the spiritual man . . . that all must be consistent with that which they preach; that what they preach they must practice; and that those who have the education in specific lines of endeavor must be consistent with the whole.

Along such lines did the entity raise the insistence in those periods; that all phases must be consistent.   1007-3

Araaraart was tested to the limits of his ability in holding his kingdom together against this complex of threats.

. . . and troublesome times arose for many, many suns, or until at least nine seasons had passed . . .   294-149

. . . the entity was in . . . Egypt, during those periods or activities when turmoils and strifes — because of personalities — had brought such confusion among the peoples of the land — when there was the chime for the recall of the Priest, as in opposition to the peoples from Atlantis and the natives and those of the household even of the King who had rebelled and brought confusion.   2397-1

Nubia

While the home kingdom was tottering on the brink of total chaos, conditions were peaceful and constructive in Nubia, the land to which Ra Ta had led two hundred and thirty-one followers.

With the entering into the Nubian land, there came such a change that there were the bettered conditions in every term that may be applied to human experience . . .   294-150

At first, the natives of Nubia resisted Ra Ta and his people, but they soon recognized this group as a boon to the development of their land.

The entity then was among the princes, being the Prince of the Nubian land. At first, with the sojourn of Ra Ta in the land, the Prince rebelled; yet — coming under the influence or associations of the companions of Ra Ta — the entity found that which brought to himself, to his land, to his peoples, a development that has stood throughout the ages — and still exists — pertaining to those mysterious abilities, through chants, through charms, to bring to the people of that land an understanding that is not readily nor easily understood by those that *call themselves* of the more excellent class or group.   416-1

The entity was among those peoples and the rulers, or the prince, of that land to which the Priest was banished. At first the entity was a resister of the tenets of the Priest; later becoming one that was a close

40

follower with the tenets of the Priest. Though in that experience those of the opposite sex were the rulers, the entity was the prince – and when the tenets of the Priest were taken, the entity – raised to power – brought much in the experience, as El-Ed-In, that made for a great advancement among the Princess' and the Prince's own peoples. 816-3

This matriarchal society of Nubians grew closer to Ra Ta and his followers. The Priest continued his teaching, and many Nubians (or Libyans) became his students.

... the entity Ai-Si was a princess among the sons of the Libyans.

When the priest Ra Ta was banished to the land, the entity came under the influences of those teachings; as the Priest dwelt there.

As would be counted in years in the present, the entity was some seventeen years of age.

The entity then joined with those that would purify their bodies for a service, in the gathering of the lessons of the Priest in such a manner that they (the lessons) might be given to others; much as the preparation, as would be termed in the day the entity became a student of the tenets that were presented by the Priest and his followers. 275-33

Various Nubians, through Ra Ta's teachings, advanced to positions of greatness.

Then the entity kept very close in touch with those developments, often going and coming to meet the Priest and those changes that came about in the political, the economic, the social or so-called religious experiences of what may be said to be the whole world during that experience.

Throughout the experience the entity gained, for he became that one that later was worshiped in that land. And the statues that are seen in that land where they have the extra arms, the extra activities, were of the entity – in his ability to minister to all phases of his own peoples during that sojourn. 816-3

At this time, Ra Ta went into relative seclusion to attune himself to the Creative Forces. He thus became more effective in channeling these forces into material projects.

As the Priest in this period entered more and more into the closer relationships with the Creative Forces, greater were the abilities for the entity or body Ra Ta to be able to make or bring about the *material* manifestations of that relationship. 294-150

Many of the exiles became Ra Ta's guards and defenders. Others interpreted the knowledge coming through Ra Ta for the people.

With the number that went in exile, of the two hundred and thirty and one souls, many were in the capacity of guards, defenders, special body-guards, interpreters – not that these interpreters were to interpret languages, or speech, or activities, but give to those that were unable to approach the Priest, or body Ra Ta, that which would be given out where it was impossible for the body to reach all about the body. 294-150

41

One individual, Ar Kar, was

. . . among those who were called the guards, or the soldiery of the Priest in banishment; remaining with him throughout that period . . . *Being*, then, close in person *to* the Priest, and one given oft to convey the messages to those whom the Priest counseled, both in exile and in old age.   1717-1

Another, Isaholli, was

. . . among those who waited upon the Priest as was banished in exile during the troublesome period. The entity among those who waited on the holy place from which the ministration of that given as moral, penal, and spiritual precept, that both from the Priest and the teacher of that period.
                                                                     69-1

The society of this exiled group continued to develop. Homes were established and family life was begun.

With these changes, there became the natural consequences in change of relationships. Pairs were given places of abode, and then homes — with their environs — were first established among those that were sent in exile, or chose of their own volition to be among that number, or who named the name of the Priest.   294-150

Building projects were started, and the following reading suggests that the volcanic energy of the mountains was tapped.

There were begun some memorials in the Nubian land which still may be seen, even in this period, in the mountains of the land. Whole mountains were honeycombed, and were dug into sufficient to where the perpetual fires are *still* in activity in these various periods . . .   295-150

Ra Ta also accomplished a great deal in the sciences, formulating knowledge of geography, astronomy, astrology, horticulture and agriculture.

. . . when the Priest then began to show the manifestations of those periods of reckoning the longitude (as termed now), latitude, and the activities of the planets and stars, and the various groups of stars, constellations, and the various influences that are held in place, or that *hold* in place those about this particular solar system. Hence in the Nubian land there were first begun the reckoning of those periods when the Sun has its influence upon human life, and let's remember that it is in this period when the *present race* has been called into being — and the *influence* is reckoned from all experiences of Ra Ta, as the effect upon the body physical, the body mental, the body spiritual, or soul body; and these are the reckonings and the effects that were reckoned with, and about, and of, and concerning, in their various phases and effects. These all were set, not by Ra Ta — but *expressed* in the *development* of Ra Ta, that these *do* affect — by the forces as set upon all — not only the inhabitant of a given sphere or planet, but the effect all has upon every form of expression in that sphere of the Creative Energies in action in that given sphere, and this particular sphere – or earth – was the *reckoning* in that period. Hence arose what some termed those idiosyncrasies of planting in the moon, or in the phases of the moon, or of the tides and their effect, or of the calling of an animal in certain phases of the moon or seasons of the year, or of the combining of elements in the mineral kingdom, vegetable kingdom, animal kingdom, in various periods, were *first* discovered – or first given, not discovered – first *conscious* of – by Ra Ta, in his first giving to the peoples of the Nubian land. 294-150

Great strides were also made in medicine, particularly by one of Ra Ta's older daughters, Aris Hobeth.

For, most of the operations through that particular experience were performed under the anaesthesia of fire – or the drug from the lotus combined with the reeds of the Nile, to prepare the bodies for the searing or burning or cutting as performed upon them.

The entity supervised much of the preparations for these. Much of the information or the guide for these was obtained by the entity in those activities during the banishment, because of the experiences of those individuals in the mountains of that land. 2329-3

Ra Ta did manage, however, to continue with Isris the activities of raising a family.

Before that we find the entity was in the Egyptian land, among the daughters of the Priest born in captivity – or in the expulsion from the land. Hence the entity grew up under the activities in the temple as one purified, before the entrance into the activities when the Priest returned. Hence the entity became as one set apart, as one worshiped – because of being the offspring of the Priest's companion in exile ... 2015-3

When those in Egypt heard of the peaceful progress made in Nubia, many realized they had made a grave mistake in banishing Ra Ta.

Well may it be imagined, then, as to the effect this had upon the peoples who classed themselves as the elect, the chosen, and yet recognizing that for a *physical* activity there had been the envy, selfishness, strife, contention, and those things that are of the body, that pertain to those lusts of the body, which had brought about or produced that which separated that which would build from themselves. 294-150

Chapter Four

THE RETURN

Peace was eventually reinstated in Egypt, but not

> . . . until there had been definite arrangements made that the Priest *would* return and all would be submissive to his mandates; and he became, then, as may be termed in the present, a dictator − or a monarch in his own right.   294-149

How was order re-established? How was Ra Ta returned to Egypt? A massive effort at conciliation was needed.

Steps in this direction began not long after the Priest was banished, with emissaries traveling between Egypt and Nubia. At one point an attempt at *forcing* a return was made, but Ra Ta was in isolation and could not be reached.

> More and more were there overtures made that there be some means provided whereby those who had followed the Priest might be *made*, or *forced*, to return; yet these became as insurmountable objections, so that only those who were acting in the capacity of go-betweens of either sex were kept, or able to be in touch with the Priest direct.   294-150

When it was learned that the Atlanteans had arrived in Egypt in force, Hept-Supht returned after only three years in Nubia. He was needed in Egypt to deal with the political conflicts created by the Atlanteans.

> . . . the return first of the Atlantean through the political influences brought to bear by the numbers of Atlanteans that were sojourning and entering into the land, as there were evidences and prophecies of Atlantis being broken up, and Egypt was chosen as one of those places where the records of that activity or peoples were to be established. Hence the Atlantean or [378] returned after only three years in banishment. And the union with the instructor and teacher, as man and wife, began much of

44

that which has been given of the messages sent to and from Egypt and
Abyssinia during the exile of the Priest.   275-38

Messengers who were neutral traveled between Egypt and Nubia,
keeping both sides informed.

In those experiences we find the entity acted in the capacities as the
informant for the King, as well as the attempted informant to those in the
banishment group. Thus we find the entity not playing the traitor to
either, but rather as one who made for those developments for each *in* the
latter part of the sojourn, or when there was the return of the Priest . . .
                                                                  1724-4

Spies from the King occasionally infiltrated the exiled group.

The entity then was among those who went *with* those peoples, as one
who would aid — rather than as a watcher or hanger-on, from the King's
command; not as a spy, neither as a tale bearer, rather as one that would
suffer *with* those . . .   1920-1

Ehel, an emissary from the King, became a close friend of Ra Ta
and joined his followers.

. . . when the entity was sent as an emissary *of* the King, or king's father,
did the entity turn to be the *friend* and the aide *to* the Priest. Termed, in
the experience, as a turncoat, or one as a spy.   99-6

As the end of this nine-year cycle approached, Araaraart brought
an end to the rebellion through both negotiation and military might.
The Oelom revolution was not ended without bloodshed.

We find with the entity [Oelom] that raised the revolution when there
was the seeming weakness in the foundation of the entity's [Araaraart's]
rule, the entity [Araaraart] in love conquered those that would over-
throw — yet might, main and blood was spent — yet in the present there is
seen, that: United powers may stand.   341-24

But understanding from some of the natives themselves also
helped. One native, Ask-Elktt, demonstrated particular wisdom in
this situation.

The entity then was among the natives who made for a drawing together rather than the separations. And there the entity gained much.
In those experiences the entity sought to make for bonds of union
rather than separations among its own peoples. Yet the love, the desire for
its own peoples to be the lead, the van [vanguard], made for misunder-
standings in the entity's experience and activity.
And it was long after the entity's departure from those experiences that
the whole purport was fully comprehended by many.
The name then was Ask-Elktt.
In the experience the entity *gained*.
And holding to those tenets of the Law of One, as to the fruits of the
spirit, was the practice and the preaching of the entity — that is:

As ye would have another be, that be thyself.
Do not ask another to do that ye would not do thyself.
Make concessions only to the weak.
Defy the strong if they are in the wrong.   1336-1

The readings suggest negotiation was necessary to stop the Ibex
rebellion:

The entity was among those of the King's command, and aided in
bringing about order among those that rebelled during the period; being
rather closely associated with the King's brother that rebelled also and set
up the kingdom or the palace in Ibex.   415-1

The natives also helped Araaraart end this rebellion.

And the *entity* joined nigh unto the King's brother who went into
activities in what was called the Ibex Rebellion.

There the entity rose in power and became as one worshiped by those
of her own groups as well as others for a period.

And when this Rebellion was broken by the activities of the natives
as well as the King, the entity then fell into what would be called — for
the experience — evil days.   1551-2

Ralij, the Prince of Ibex, met his fate in banishment:

. . . and only in the *banishment* of the Ibex ruler did there again become
that of a period of rest to the entity.   23-1

Although the war with the Ibex was concluded, differences remained — and this conflict would flare up again at a later period.

The political disagreements with the Atlanteans were ended
through arbitration, possibly due to Hept-Supht and the efforts of
those members of the Law of One who did not favor Ax-Tell's
ambitions.

Ix-enl, a companion of Ax-Tell, became a helpful influence in the
arbitration, serving as a judge.

The entity then, as a companion of Ax-Tell, became the leader in
those activities when there was begun the correlation of the experiences of
those peoples when the turmoils and strifes arose.

And the entity aided much in the clearing of differences, and in
establishing those activities that made for the greater understandings of all
the different purposes, or the different presentations of purposes in that
period.   1035-1

. . . the entity was in the Egyptian land, among the Atlanteans who
were active when there were the attempts of unifying the varied groups
when there was the return of the Priest to authority in partially a religious
sense and partially a political sense, but more in the moral way and in the
preparation of individuals for special or definite services in the land.
                    5008-1

Now that differences were being settled, Ra Ta's return was petitioned by many different groups.

Hence there were overtures made to the ruler, and to those in authority with same, that the Priest be recalled. 281-43

Those individuals who had been purified in the temples and remained true to Ra Ta's teaching during his absence began to use their influence. Their prayers and meditations were for peace and the Priest's return.

The entity then was among those that were raised to high position in that of the dancer, or entertainer in the temple; suffering much with the dissensions as arose . . . and close associate of the High Priest as was banished, and became one that aided especially in the return of the Priest [294] and the one [538] chosen as companion; aiding in making for a better understanding in the social or moral relationships in the new conditions arising. 454-2

. . . those that were advanced in their purification in the temple — whether they were of the male or female, *with* the ideal of bringing peace to their friends, their peoples, to whom they held some allegiance, kept attempting to make for such associations with the Council and the King that there be the re-establishing of the Priest in his place in the land. 294-150

Several members of the Council also joined in the effort for recalling the exiles.

The entity was of the councilors who were appealed to by the natives that had been in rebellion, and aided in correlating with the Atlanteans as well as the general populace the reasons *for* the recall . . . 2834-1

The entity was a councilor to the young King . . . Then the entity was in the name Arar-apth.
When the rebellions arose, the activities of the entity were to counsel with the King, being among those that aided in the re-establishing of the Priest upon the return . . . 478-1

For the entity was among those of the councilors to the King — but of the natives — and of the young King.
In the name then Sil-At-Bell, the entity gained; for while there were those turmoils and strifes, the abilities of the entity were to keep counsel, not only with the King but with those who made the preparations for the considerations of the return of the Priest . . . 1188-2

Even the member of the King's Command who had negotiated an Ibex settlement urged Araaraart to return Ra Ta.

The entity was among those of the King's Command . . . [and] brought to the attention of the King the necessities for the return of the Priest, or the peoples, to the mental and religious activities, that there might be established a united kingdom again. 415-1

Finally the old king, Arart, asserted his influence. His aid was requested by the mother of the Scribe, and Ra Ta himself.

The entity then among those that counseled with the ruler, being the *father* of that ruler who set the house in order . . . being among those that counseled for the return of the Priest and the re-establishing of the school or church . . .   165-2

The entity then was the mother of that native [Aarat], that rose as one to be pitted against the younger king; in the name then — as would be determined or called in the present — She-Telle.

In the experience the entity gained. For only in the latter portion did the entity become able to aid in making it possible for the King (the old king) to bring about a harmonious gathering over and above the activities of the son and those that were in charge of the buildings and the activities that made for the material progresses during that portion of the experience.   1438-1

Q-5. Who was that individual "sought out" by the Priest to aid him?
A-5. The former King, who entered with his people into the Egyptian experience — as has been indicated heretofore.   281-44

Ra Ta soon learned of the movement in his behalf.

The entity then was one that counseled with the ruler and the Priest, bringing the first of the messages to the Priest of the *possibility* of the return . . .   295-1

But the turmoils and the hard work in Nubia had drained Ra Ta, and he had aged rapidly. Many feared that he would not be able to carry on.

In this condition, then, were there emissaries of the various positions sent back and forth by the leaders of that particular period, that would eventually bring about the restoring of the Priest, who — under the *strain* — in a very short period had, to the apparent eye of those about him, became aged, decrepit, and not able physically to carry on; and *fear* began to be felt that there would not be the sustaining strength sufficient that there might be given to the peoples that which had been begun by the entity in the Egyptian land, and that which was being manifested in this land to which they had been banished.   294-150

Although he was weak in body, Ra Ta

. . . was strong in the power of mind and in the abilities to correlate the truths that had been and were gathered for the dispensing of the knowledge and understanding gained to the peoples in the period . . .
                                                       1925-1

Preparation for Ra Ta's return proceeded.

Eventually came the period when there was to be the attempt, that there was to be the return of the Priest to the land.   294-150

It was at this time that Ra Ta arranged to have "marks" set in the bodies of those who were, or would be, close to him and his teachings. These physical signs would appear on the bodies of that group from lifetime to lifetime, as its members were drawn together by that Egyptian association.

Then did this Priest of himself, and of the Creative Forces, *edict* that those who were in close association with this entity — that had meant an extenuation or savior of a peoples, into a regeneration of same — would have marks set in their bodies that would remain throughout their appearance in the earth's plane, that they might be known to one another, would they seek to know the closer relationships of the self to the Creative Forces and the *source* — *physical* — of *their* activity *with* that source. To some in the eye, to some in the body, to some the marks upon the body, in those ways and manners that may only be known to those that are in that physical and spiritual attunement with the entity as they pass through the material or earth's sphere together. They are drawn, then, by what? That same element that was being accentuated in the earth's plane, as also the other laws that were discovered — or were given, or were conscious of — by the entity in that particular period. The purpose of such, then, that there may be known, that with such an association there may come an awakening to that which was accomplished by those of the select — not elect, but *select* — in that particular endeavor.

294-150

For, as given in that respecting the influence, the teaching of the Priest, there was left with each entity a mark, either in body as expressed physically or in the name, that they each are called in their experiences.

275-38

Q-1. Was I given a mark by Ra Ta? If so, where is it, and what is the meaning of it?

A-1. The upper portion of the lip, or between the nasal passages and the corner of the lip — which exists there at times — especially a feeling of twitching there: the messenger, the speaker to those that need counsel and advice.

1100-26

Q-14. What mark was given me by Ra Ta in Egypt, if any?

A-14. The mark on the body, as in the lower portion of the left shoulder blade; indicating ever the holding up of those purposes to which the entity gave itself in its activity in that experience; of giving — through the best of itself — the strength of its body, its mind, its soul-purpose.

2829-1

When the return was effected, a hundred and sixty-seven followers accompanied Ra Ta. Others of the original party remained, while many Nubians (or Abyssinians) left their home and entered Egypt.

The Atlanteans assisted the expedition:

Q-6. In what kind of vehicles did the Priest and his retinue return to Egypt after the banishment?

49

A-6. In what would be called chariots driven by the gases; for the Atlanteans prepared those that brought these back. The followers were on the camels and the animals that were used in the service during that period. The camel, the donkey, the horse were later in this land, and introduced by the Arabians.   275-38

Ceremonies and rejoicing greeted the expedition.

As the Priest, Ra Ta, with his retinue or his companions were brought back to the kingdom there was much rejoicing on the part of many of the peoples, and — as would be termed in the present — rather the gala occasion, and the priest, Ra-La-Ral, with the peoples that had become adherents to the faith of the Priest in the banishment led the way with the king's own guard, see? while the household of the Priest with those that were in attendance to same were among those in the closer association with the Priest; the Priest acting in the capacity of the leader in the experience and the entity — as the Priest's son — accepted or received the priest [Ra-La-Ral] at the place of abode, and here the meeting in the experience of the entity with the one becoming the entity's companion [301]. The embrace, the kisses in this meeting, were as the making for the entity — in the sight of that as was preached or given by him — the joining them in the union as one.

The entity at this time or period was in years what would today be called eighteen, while the bride — as would be called, or the half-sister that was accepted as the companion — was only eight.   282-7

Osis, who had chosen exile, now became Araaraart's wife.

. . . and with the return to the position in the later days raised to that position of the wife to the King, and the mother of the heir to the throne, who builded most of those tombs that are being shown today.   2486-1

There was still the question of what position Ra Ta would now occupy in the religious and political establishments. No one desired further conflict.

With the advent or the entering of the individual groups from other lands, as well as the overtures from the many for the return of the Priest (and the entity's parent), there were periods of fear — because of those conditions which had existed in the association, and as to what was to be the association with the return of the Priest to at least the religious power (as would be termed in the present), and the ability of the Priest to produce or make for many of the political situations, as would be termed in the present.   1100-26

Ra Ta's immediate need was to strengthen his body.

With the return then of the Priest to the Temple Beautiful, there first began the Priest to withdraw himself from the whole that regeneration in body might become manifest, and the body lay down the material weaknesses — and from those sources of regeneration *recreated* the body in its *elemental* forces for the carrying on of that which these material positions gave the opportunity for . . .   294-150

This rejuvenation meant a washing away of the physical manifestations of all the years of turmoil. One named Apt-hen underwent this process with Ra Ta.

> For the entity aided the Priest during those periods when the regeneration of the body came to him through the casting aside, as it were, of the years of toil and strife through which the body of Ra Ta itself had passed; and the entity rejuvenated itself with that body in the experience; rising in the latter portion of the sojourn to those conditions wherein it was given entire *charge of* the activities in the *temples* of Sacrifice, or the temples of initiation — where there were those things carried on in the tombs that were prepared for such during those periods of activity.   696-1

> The Priest in body, as has been given, in the height of the development was at the regeneration, or when over a hundred years (or light years) in the earth. Six feet one inch tall, weighing — what in the present would be called — a hundred and eighty-one pounds. Fair of face, not too much hair on the head nor too much on the face or body. In color nearly white, only sun or air tanned.   275-38

Ra Ta's regeneration dispelled the doubts and fears about his position. The nation was

> . . . submissive to his mandates; and he became, then, as may be termed in the present, a dictator — or a monarch in his own right.   294-149

> . . . with the recall of the Priest and the activities of those peoples from Atlantis, order in a form had been restored — and there began the period of expansion.   2533-4

RECONSTRUCTION

Politics

The need for political change was obvious.

> In the portion as may be termed the political, with this return — and the necessary changes or alterations in the various sections of this division of the peoples — many changes came about; for, as we find, the native counselor [Aarat] was rather in the position of the subordinate to the King's demands, or the demands of the *father* of the King, and became rather as a recluse, and shut from much of the activities that were being carried on in the relationships of the nations or peoples with the outside peoples.   294-151

After her return from exile, Isris, now called Isis, was raised to a position of national leadership. Many who wished to gain access to the throne had to do so through Isis.

This, then, made for an *endowing* of . . . [Isis] to the position of the first goddess that was so crowned, and there was given then that place that was to be sought by others that would gain counsel and advice even from the Priest, gained access through that of Isis to the Throne itself. Not that it rose above the authority of the King, but for that developing necessary for the activities of the woman in those spheres of activity in this particular development.   294-151

Tkelupan, the son of Raai, had been active in the rebellions and remained dissatisfied with the new regime. Therefore, he moved to the extreme south of Egypt and established his own kingdom, which was continually at odds with the North.

. . . the entity was . . . the son of the king deposed by those groups that came in from the Persian land or Carpathia led by the Priest.

These made for combative experiences with the entity, for the entity attempted to arouse various natives to rebellion. With the ceasing of the rebellions, the entity went into a portion of the upper country or the southernmost portions of Egypt; and established a kingdom of its own.

The activities were ever at variance with those influences wrought by the developings in the Egyptian land, and in the later portion of the entity's experience there were overtures made that eventually − in the second generation of the entity's experience − brought the undermining of the attempts of Ra Ta in that land.   3189-2

With strong leadership the state began again to progress.

. . . for these were being guided by a ruler or king whose authority was not questioned any more, nor were the advisings of the Priest questioned . . .   299-151

Society

One of the first projects of reconstruction was the re-establishment of homes and family life:

. . . there began then the segregations more into places, homes, and where there had only been forts or temples in the various sections − where the various character of commercial life was carried on − gradually grew homes, with families, that were much in the order as may be found in the present day, save there were more than one companion in the various households.   294-151

The entity . . . aided in establishing homes, which became to the entity as a unit of filial love, in which marital relationships might be born through those periods when so changed.   3474-1

Many people were involved in the building of homes including Ra Ta's brother, Gud-El-On. Previously he had sided against the Priest but, having made his repentance, was now supplying materials for the project.

Then there were the closer activities, following his repentance, or his *accepting* of those activities for the supplying of materials for the temples, or for the King's household and the homes and the buildings of same.

2345-1

Much of the impetus behind these activities came from the Atlanteans, particularly Ax-Tell and Ajax, who were familiar with this style of living and building.

Among those activities, as we have intimated, there was the establishing of homes — which was an outcome or a growth, or an unfoldment, from those experiences that had caused the banishment of the Priest. These also were a part of the activities that had been suggested or propounded from the leaders Ax-Tell and Ajax from the Atlantean land, as had been a part of the experience that had brought about the greater bettering of feeling and the manifestation of a unity among those peoples in Atlantis before its final destruction.

2533-4

The entity . . . being of those peoples from the Atlantean land. And with the training and the tenets of the Law of One, those things pertaining to that which first brought the conveniences in the lives of those that were home builders . . .

1150-1

The entity then was the first of the Atlantean peoples *born* in the Egyptian land; or the mother of the entity then was heavy with child when the entity entered into the land now known as Egypt . . . And the entity was what *today* would be termed a prodigy, in that experience.

Then in the name Atlenteus [?], the entity rose to power . . .

The entity became then the overseer or supervisor of many of the buildings that were set up during the experience; as the Atlanteans had been among those who made themselves temples and homes of stone and wood, and dealt with such activities.

984-1

The following reading describes some of the houses of this period:

Q-2. Please describe the family life and mode of living during the Egyptian incarnation.

A-2. As is known, the peoples who entered in were rather tent dwellers; while the natives had been among those who, for the greater portion of their sojourn, had builded houses — that were low in height, which made for the preservation or protection during those seasons that necessitated the coverings, not only for the cold but for the rainy seasons there — as has ever been. Yet the greater portion of the home life and its activity was carried on in what might now be termed as the roof, or the outer activity was upon the roof of the dwellings. These were builded, as it were, close together in various groups, or the various families or various tribes.

These were the manners of the life.

798-4

Under Isis' leadership, and along with the development of homes, women were able to attain advanced positions in the society.

. . . these changed the position or attitude of these particular peoples as to the position that was held by woman in her relations to the developing of the conditions that either were to be national, local, or individual; for not only does this become then that upon which man depends for those advancements or advents into the material activities, but the nourishing of, the maintaining of, that to which its (the man's) ideals are to be turned in their activity when they arise at that period when expressions are to be given to the active forces in the material activities.   294-151

Perhaps Isis had become impressed with the matriarchal rule in Nubia. She may also have been responding to an ancient tradition in the Nile Valley, for in primeval Egypt (10,500,000 B.C.) women had been the rulers of society.

Q-12. Was I a man at the time when among those that put up the first of the pyramids?
A-12. Then there was rather that as a woman, the entity was the ruler over those of man — and had many men as husbands, then.   993-3

Os-is-el, one of the daughters of Ra Ta and Isis born in exile, also worked for the advancement of women.

In the experience the entity brought much of that which aided womankind, all of her sex, in greater activity; as did the entity in the sojourn just before the present bring to her fellows an aid towards freedom of speech, as well as the privilege of owning, holding possessions in the own name.   2015-3

Economy

When order was restored, the nation's economy began to flourish. Granaries and storehouses were re-established and foreign trade began.

. . . the entity then was a supervisor over the granaries, the storehouses of gold, the storehouses for the precious stones, the divisions of those things that were to go to those in power or authority for the sustaining of the land, and for the propagation and distribution of knowledge as might be of a helpful nature.   1574-1

The entity then was among those who set about to be in charge over what we would call the granaries, or those places for the preservation of the grains of the land, and the dealing of same out to other lands where they were given in exchange for spices from some, perfumes from others, gold from others, and certain characters of animals from others.   1587-1

A system of credit distribution was instated.

. . . the entity was active as to judgments of commodities of various districts, and their needs, and the credit as administered for the various groups that were employed in such for the supplying of the needs for the greater number of people of the land.   2399-1

Insurance and social security projects were set up. Ex-der-enemus, referred to as the "father of insurance," was the first one to recognize the people's need for financial security.

And with the establishing of the homes, and the environs or surroundings of same, there came about those periods when there were losses by the natural sources, or nature — fire, lightning, floods and the like, as well as death — that hindered, or caused the needs for the State to become responsible for the activities of the individual groups who became dependent upon such sources or natures.   2533-4

Ex-der-enemus then conceived the idea of a collective insurance policy and convinced Araaraart, Ra Ta, and the Atlantean leaders of the plan's desirability.

Thus those activities as might be called the first purposes, as well as the father of insurance, or assurance, to groups, to individuals, were a part of this entity's labors; collaborating same with the ruler — or the secular ruler, or the king, Araaraart, as well as with the Priest and those rulers that had been in authority through that experience in the Atlantean land.

2533-4

This cooperative endeavor was worked out in detail:

. . . the entity presented the first idea as to how there might be assurances to individual families as to how their own affairs, their own homes, their own farms, their own places of business, their own choice of the selective work, might be carried on, by groups contributing to a general fund that was handled by the individual entity; and there was the license given to each group — with certain numbers to be applied to each group, and each contributing so much to the welfare. Thus the whole sum was given to those to whom such assurance was given for protection; as to life expectancy and as to incidents or accidents or things that caused losses to such individual groups.   2533-4

There was specific insurance for various fraternal groups, or what might be termed the first labor unions:

Thus, what might be called the assurance, or insurance, of fraternal activities was also a part of those groups. For, these were combined into those groups that were workers with the State, workers with the teaching, or those who administered, or the farmers of grain, as well as the makers of paper, the builders of homes, the builders for the State. Each of these groups had a form of assurance, or insurance; which was in the form or manner of the first unions, as would be called today.   2533-4

Ra Ta, Araaraart, Ax-Tell, and Ajax made up the governing board which issued suggestions to the various national unions.

. . . these formed what might be called today the board, or governing board, or suggestive board, to those various groups or unions — that carried not only the means or manners of preparing individuals who maintained or retained activity in this individual form of service in whatever field had been chosen, but selected them to become active individuals — from those who showed their aptness in certain forms of service; as in the diplomatic service, or in the exchange with other nations or states or groups with which there was being formed some character of relationship.

2533-4

This insurance program was founded on the precepts of a communalistic economy. Each member contributed to the betterment of the whole; the profit motive was not a part of the system.

These worked together for the betterment of the *whole*, and not for individual exploitation of the so-called capitalists. For, there were not such in those experiences. For, as was the custom in a land that the entity became a part of, or is at present — those that worked not didn't eat — save those that were disabled or who had not come to the age of accountability for their own supply, or for their activity . . . And thus came the forming of groups for that particular form of service. And as these worked, so came the unfoldment of the other forms of cooperative activity. But all free peoples, see?

Q-2. What methods were employed then to interest and cause individuals and groups to participate in these plans of insurance protection?
A-2. It was the natural thing that each individual group sought to better themselves in their particular vocation or activity, to be able to supply in their activities that needed for the betterment of the peoples as a whole. It was activity from that angle of a self-interest, yes — but also of a national interest, or the abilities of the group to excel in whatever field of activity was chosen.

It was not necessary to interest. While it was not compulsory, but each individual — as it unfolded — was seeking to better self, as well as the particular vocation chosen — for it was considered in relationship with the whole effort of the government itself . . .

There was no competition, then; for each group had its own individual form of activity, and coordinated same with the whole. 2533-4

Another reading tells us that in this period there was "the founding of communistic ideas from which much of the Christian era thought was built." (38-1)

We should note something about longevity in that period, since it certainly has a bearing on insurance programs. Initially, there was little need for insurance; people lived hundreds of years. Later, people began to "lay aside the outer shell" after what we would consider a normal life-span. This was done by assignment and/or choice.

To be sure, in the beginning there was little of that we term today as life insurance, or assurance. For, the life expectancy in those periods extended over a hundred, and hundreds of years; and thus these were not accounted for, but rather there were those groups that chose to lay aside the outer shell when the life expectancy — as would be termed in the present — was completed, as it had been laid out by those who gave the assignment, or the activity as was chosen by the individual. Or, there was chosen by the individual that period or particular part of the experience that was its contribution to the life of the period — and this was outlined or given. 2533-4

The entity remained in that way of activity through the experience until, in the terms as would be called in years, some four hundred and fifty and four [454] years. 1472-10

The entity's experience in the life was that of many, many, *many* years, if it would be counted by the years of today — it being more than six hundred years — yes, season years — that is, the seasons from winter to winter, or spring to spring, or summer to summer. 1100-26

Technology

. . . remember, there is nothing in the present that hasn't existed from the first. Only the *form* or the manner of its use being changed, and many an element then used that the art of its use has been lost, as we will see the reason why, and many being re-discovered by those called scientists in the present when in that day it was the common knowledge of the most illiterate, as would be termed in the present. 294-148

Technology during the Reconstruction received a boost from the Atlanteans. Ax-Tell's son, Ax-Entol, was a supervisor of storehouses and a construction engineer.

The entity was young in years when brought in, and of the household — and the son — of Ax-Tell; being of those Atlanteans who made for such great changes in the conditions and affairs and the peoples in the land . . .

The entity, then, was in the position of what would be called the engineer in the broader sense. Not only the engineer in being able to lay out the lands, the construction of bridges and viaducts and ships and things or activities that made for the preservation of same, but in the holy things — or in the building of the altars in the Temple of Sacrifice and in the Temple Beautiful.

Then the name was Ax-Entol. 1574-1

Pek-Al, who journeyed from Atlantis by air, achieved fame for his engineering of the Nile River.

The entity was among the children of the Law of One — the mathematician, the one who made preparations for those journeys through the air to the Pyrenees; later, with those establishings of the activities in Egypt, the entity took residence there; becoming associated with Ajax or Ax-Tell in those experiences.

In the name then Pek-Al, the entity made measurements for some of those activities that brought about the buildings in parts of the Nile, as to make for the governing of the waters of same.

These activities brought fame . . .   2677-1

Another Atlantean, Ax-Tenuel, "made for those developments in the chemical and electrical appliances in the experience." (1135-1)

Hept-Supht's many involvements included technological advancements:

> . . . then the entity began to work with the Priest in bringing order out of the general chaos that existed through these troublesome turmoils and periods; and aided the most in directing those that began to be the heads of the varied departments in the establishing of the truths or tenets, or practical application *of* the laws (as would be termed in the present) pertaining to those things that made for chemistry, building, commerce, labor, economic conditions, then the schools, the educational centers, and the varied activities that would be classified in such experiences in the present day.   378-13

Stone carving was developed and refined to an art form.

> . . . the entity was in that now known as the Egyptian land, among those peoples that journeyed to Egypt from that known as the Atlantean land . . . [and] was in that position, from that expected and also the developments materially, to aid the more in counseling with those who carved precious stones, those who set about work with the semi-precious and the regular building stones . . .   984-1

> Then in the name of Zeous. The entity siding then with the deposed Priest, and losing favor with the King for the amount of enthusiasm shown for the Priest — yet in the settling of these conditions, we find there were buildings and buildings built or prepared, or dedicated to this great builder.   419-1

Scientific and psychic studies were not differentiated in that period as they are today. Mathematics, geometry, and building were coordinated with astrology and divination.

> The entity then was in the name of Arsrha and was the stone and the precious stone designer and carver for that entity, the ruler, Araaraart. The entity also gave the geometrical forces to the people, being then the mathematician, and an assistant to the astrologer and soothsayer of the day.   195-14

When an Atlantean named Ajax-ol became a research partner with a member of the King's household named Asphar, the most significant technological advancements of the period were made.

Asphar was a member of the original Caucasian invaders; and a loyal friend of Araaraart.

> During that era when the Second or Young King was put in authority, as one pitted against or to bring about the cooperation with some of the natives and their activities — the entity then was among those who had

come from the Persian or Caucasian land, being an armor bearer or a personal guard to the King.

When those disputations arose among the advisors to the King, over those conditions arising with the Priest and those of that group, the entity still remained as one loyal to the King; not only then the personal guard but the friend and associate and advisor to the King; being near of the same age and of the same group or family.   470-33

Asphar met Ajax-ol through the Atlantean leader Ax-Tell. As a result of this meeting he became interested in electricity and metallurgy.

Being interested in every form of activity that might bring better conditions for individuals or groups, the entity was interested in those tales or experiences told by Ax-Tell; and sought demonstrations and experimentations with those influences which had been a part of the experience of the Atlanteans that brought about destructive influences . . .

But during that period a great deal of the time of Asphar and Ajax-ol was devoted to the use of the electrical forces maintained from the use of static forces, as called today. And in their attempts to demonstrate or use these influences for a helpfulness rather than as they had been used upon nature or individuals, or those activities of a destructive nature, these were turned to minerals. Thus the conditions in which there were the abilities for the fusion of copper and brass with the alloy that comes from gold impregnated with arsenic, with the casting of electrical forces through same. This brought those abilities of sharpening or using such metals as these for cutting instruments. . .

Q-2. Describe in detail the construction and purpose of the more important machines used by me then.

A-2. As indicated, the machine in which there was the combining of metals in those periods of fusing or smelting — that combined them in such ways that they might be used in forms not used today.

Especially the use of electrical forces with the character of instruments in operations, as well as the fusion of such metals indicated.   470-33

The readings suggest that, as armor bearer to the King, Asphar used these techniques in preparing his ruler's defense.

. . . the entity made preparations for a part of the armor, or part of the defense; as the armor bearer or the protector for the activities of the King.

All of these activities then became a part of the use of electrical forces for metals and their activity upon same to be used as carbonizing them, or directing them in manners in which they became as magnetic forces for the applications to portions of the body for transmuting or changing the *effect* of activities upon the physical energies and forces of the body; able to use same as re-ionizing or re-generating the bodily forces themselves.

470-22

This was probably the method employed by Ra Ta in his regeneration.

Chapter Five

THE TEMPLES

Twenty years passed between the time of the banishment and the re-establishment of the Temples.

The entity was the chief of those in the temple service that made for the *offerings* to a portion of the peoples. The entity gained through the experience, not deserting the temple service even when broken by the deposed Priest, nor altering the tenets – though suffering much in rebukes and temptations under the changes made, until the restoration of the temple service some twenty years later.   1923-1

When the Temple Beautiful and Temple of Sacrifice were at the height of their activity they functioned as an integral part of the society, regulating the divisions of labor, family planning, education, medical research, hospitals and spiritual ministry.

Family Planning

An important aspect of establishing homes was the purification of individuals chosen to become parents. An attempt was being made throughout the society to eliminate animal appendages in future offspring, and to improve the genetic line in general. In short, this was a program of family planning, and was coordinated with the activities of the Temples of Beauty and Sacrifice.

In the period there were those activities that possibly were at the height of the period of the Priest; having established the activities in the Temple of Sacrifice, where individuals – as might be termed – were regenerated, or had so prepared their bodies that their offspring were free from those appendages, those varied activities.   2390-7

Also there were those experiences in which families, groups and individuals had offered themselves as channels through which there would be the regeneration of the race, by the experiences of those who were chosen as channels — or parents — by their activities through the Temple of Sacrifice. These were activities to eradicate such as might be called disease and disturbances that might become hindrances to the body itself in the preparation for fatherhood or motherhood.   2533-4

For it is the indication of the entity's sacrificing its own petty conditions, or those urges which existed when the entity desired that these be purged that the body, as a channel, might bear offspring that would be purified in a physical sense.   585-10

Aris Hobeth, Ra Ta's daughter, worked with sex education:

The entity chose not an active force other than as a demonstration in the relationships to others through the sex relations, for the preparations of the body for the new form, the new expression.   2329-3

The need for physical purification continued to be emphasized:

. . . as those periods advanced for the purifying of others for definite service as well as the purifying of those in their *bodily* conditions for the preparations to become either artisans, teachers, ministers, or to fill those offices as would be termed in the present as the leaders or directors of the peoples throughout the period.   1100-26

Medicine

The Temple of Sacrifice also began to serve as a center for medical research. Here again, Atlantean techniques contributed to progress.

The entity then was among the peoples that were of *One* in Atlantis, that journeyed to Egypt and aided in those establishments of the experimentations that dealt with the principles of plant *and* animal, rather than mineral, as to the applications of these principles to the curative forces in human ills; and may. be said to have been upon the staff of the hospitalizations that were established during that building up in that period . . . While the abilities in the gathering of data, or experimental data in the application of much as may be termed as drugs in the present, were used in such work by the entity, and while to the world the entity meant much — to *self* the development was not beyond reproach.   490-1

Hence, as Shen-Phti, the entity was among those who headed or who chose to be in the group for the hospitalizations, the study of medicine . . .
                    982-4

Medical knowledge was recorded and catalogued:

And the aids to the body and mind were catalogued, or recorded, in what might be called the first concentrated efforts towards presenting hospitals, camps, or places of refuge for the ill.   441-1

As with science, medicine was closely allied with what we now call "psychic" or parapsychological studies.

. . . the entity was in the Egyptian land, when the activities of the entity brought about much of that experienced in the present through intuition, or the ability of the mind to control matter, in its dealings with others in their biological development.   3474-1

Healing techniques were expanded and now included:

1. Control of the diet.

Then the entity showed an aptitude and an ability in those directions of purification by the acts of individuals, as related to the feeding and the preparation of the various compounds of food . . .

When there became the necessity of establishing the temples where there were the studies of the combinations of diet — as in purifying the body from the blood, and the smearing of the flesh took on such activities as to remove scourges that arose from certain characters of diet; and there were brought through the feedings more symmetrical and harmonious proportions in the bodies of those that were in thought or work or service among those that prepared themselves — the entity Ai-Si began to be among the leaders in such activities . . .   275-33

2. Drugs.

The entity became one that might be termed today the alchemist or the druggist, as would be set for the hospitalizations during that experience; for the entity enjoined self with those particular activities, for its knowledge not only of people and the administering of those tendencies necessary for the aiding of those that were ill but for the knowledge of those things in the field that may be made a portion of such application — in the name then Asptha.   872-1

3. Surgery.

. . . the Temple of Sacrifice — in which there were the first operative measures performed, as would be called at present.   2329-3

. . . the entity was in the Egyptian land when there were those activities which had to do with the Temple of Sacrifice.

Then the entity was what today would be called a bleeder, or one who operated with certain activities for the removal of appendages for some of the beings or individuals of that period.   3478-2

4. Blood purification.

. . . for much was given by the entity in building for those who *suffered* in body, in the building of the school and the learning of medicine; for the entity became the first of those who bled peoples to count their blood clots.   99-6

[The entity] counseled with the Priest in the experience — requiring the periods of long meditation, from which all of the physical activities were at naught, so far as food or the material activities were concerned, but meditating upon the effects of the various influences that arose in a heterogeneous grouping, and the effect of blood purification as exemplified in daily life . . .   1100-26

5. Music therapy.

Then, as there may be seen, the attuning of the music as may be in the day; the viola tuned to the vibrations of the fires of nature may be destructive or smothering or aflaming same. So in that Temple of Sacrifice did thou minister there, in the purity of thy body, in the abilities of thy self to aid those that offered themselves in those manners of purifying; that burned away not only the desires of the flesh but the appendages of same that marred their bodies. And thus through much of thine effort came forth man as he walks upright today; no longer with the feet as of the cloven ox; or the horns as of the roe, the goat; nor the hog; nor those that would make themselves as a tree, nor those whose bodies were alive with the serpents of wisdom. But rather in the godly sons of the sons of God that wasted not their wanton selves in the mire of despair with the sons of men but kept the faith; as thou — in thy purifying of same — made for those vibrations that in the music as of the spheres brought that purifying through attuning the vibrations with the destructive forces as manifested themselves in nature, as *tore away* in matter that which hindered the individual, the soul, from knowing and being at-one with that Creative Force as thou had gained and did manifest in that experience.   275-43

6. Athletics.

Again we find those expressions in the experience of the entity when there should be the developments of the body towards what would be called today athletics, and those activities which were then as the preservation and dedicating of the body to the Divine or to purposes for the better expressions in material worlds.   1346-1

The most significant advances in medical techniques occurred when Asphar, Ajax and Ajax-ol applied their discoveries in electricity and metallurgy to healing.

Those activities made for closer associations, for then Ajax — or [487] — and the entity now called [470] made the application or use of the abilities in engineering, and the building of machines for the application of these to the bodies of individuals — where there were appurtenances to be left off, where there was blood to be changed, or where the vibratory forces were to be set so as to remove those influences of possessions; and where there were those activities in which with the combination of sodas the bodily forces were enabled to reproduce in a manner as cross to that to which it had been set in its natural forces.   470-22

An electrical knife was developed for bloodless surgery:

Also there were those activities and abilities of the entity to use the electrical devices as prepared through those periods of their investigation, for operative measures; wherein the electrical knife was in such a shape, with the use of the metals, as to be used as the means for bloodless surgery, as would be termed today — by the very staying forces used which formed coagulating forces in bodies where larger arteries or veins were to be entered or cut.

Then, such were the greater activities of the entity through those influences which had to do especially with the Temple of Sacrifice.

470-33

Then ye applied the electrical forces, as some of the associates became able to use the electrical knife in the surgery that was taught and practiced there.

3333-1

The following extract explains the philosophy behind this medical technique:

For as the very forces of the bodily functionings are electrical in their activity, the very action of assimilation and distribution of assimilated forces is in the physical body an active force of the very *low* yet very high *vibratory* forces themselves.

Hence there the entity made application in those directions; and these act upon the influences or forces or metals, or active principles within the human forces themselves.

For within the human body – living, not dead – *living* human forces – we find every element, every gas, every mineral, every influence that is outside of the organism itself. For indeed it is one with the whole. For it is not only a portion of, and equal to, and able to overcome or meet every influence within, but there is not the ability in the third dimensional force or influence to even imagine anything that isn't a part of the activity of a physical *living* organism!

470-22

Electrical surgery was an integral part of the program dedicated to the purification of the race.

Hence the use of these was a portion of the entity's experience, when there was the preparation for the cleansing and the transmuting of the bodies in the preparations for the new race.

470-22

Education

The Temple Beautiful and the Temple of Sacrifice, together, became in the original meaning of the word, a university. As a *temple*-university it was more than a collection of colleges, and although it did incorporate intellectual activities, its overall purpose was to synthesize knowledge.

All the arts and sciences, channeled through the temples, were applied to a united cultural effort towards the highest spiritual ideal – a realization of Oneness on the planet Earth. This university, with its clearly defined purposes, was fully integrated with the dynamics of daily life.

The temples regulated the total range of education, from elementary to college level.

. . . in the restoration and the building up of the emissaries' activities the entity then assumed charge of the *younger* ones' activity in the temple, and in the school, making same as compatible with the physical life and the moral life – as related to the tenets of those as taught during that experience. 1922-1

Thus the entity will find in the present the interest in building in the hearts of the young, through those activities that may bring hope and those activities of the correct directing that were a part of the activities during that particular period; by those activities of what would be called the school . . . 1438-1

. . . there came that which made in the latter days for a period of service to those peoples – especially in the capacity of what would be termed in the present as the nurse, the teacher, the instructor to those of the young, to those in teen ages . . . 1182-1

And then there were the teachings and education through the Temple Beautiful, which would be the same as represented in today's universal school or college or institution of learning. 2533-4

Pseudal, a native priest, was leader of the State's education:

. . . and the entity gained in the period by the teachings as were given to the peoples; aiding in the establishment of the school (as may be termed in this present day parlance), for the entity became the *leader* in the *school* movement, and broadening the field of the endeavor *through* the application of the religious forces as applied to material life, of the material things as applied to the spiritual life, of the secular things in life as applied to the mental *influences* in peoples of the period. In the name Pseudal. 957-1

Atlanteans also contributed to the growth of education.

The entity then, of the daughters of the Law of One, came with Ajax, came with those who became as the leaders in establishing with the Priest of the Egyptian land those activities in which the individuals were fitted for special service owing to their individual faculties and developments for individual service.

There the entity was as a head of the departments of what ye would call education, and the activities for the various services in the land; and the giving of the tenets to others. 1554-2

A variety of subjects was taught in the Temple Beautiful, many of which are familiar to the student of today.

. . . in the establishing of the rules, in the establishing of the schools, in the establishing of the distribution of those forces as man applied in what became religious thought, what became the aiding in the physical body, those as became the schooling of the mental forces and the understanding of the relationships of man to man, and man to the creative forces. The entity aided in that school . . . 1735-2

Oelom, the native leader who had revolted against Araaraart, now served as a teacher of education and music:

. . . the entity rose to the position of being an instructor in not only much of what would be called educational factors and features in the experiences of the period, but in the musical talents or activities of others as well.   849-45

Other subjects included psychology and medicine:

Q-12. What did the entity teach in its Egyptian incarnation?
A-12. The correlating of the activities of individuals in the material affairs with the *coordinating* of same in the *spiritual* affairs of the individual; or, as would be termed in the present, that of an economic psychologist — in that particular period.   488-6

Then the entity was a teacher, a lecturer; aiding those that made for the developings of that later to become known as the *beginning* of the *physical* healing to or for *bodily* ills.   980-1

. . . the entity was raised to the position of supervisor over the distributions of the lessons that were gained through the establishments of the schools, both for the development of the applications for physical ills and the developments for the creating of the fires in the soul and the material affairs of individuals.   692-1

One of the more interesting subjects was prophecy or divination.

Thus we find that all prophecy, all forms of those that would prophesy or make or leave or portend experiences, are of special interest to the entity; as these were a part of the entity's activity — as a student rather than as an active force — through that experience.
The entity was acquainted with all those in various forms of authority — which brought satisfaction in a manner, or rather the ability of the entity to become the greater student through that experience.   2823-1

The Temple of Sacrifice also had "seats of learning" which corresponded to the signs of the zodiac. This would indicate that astrology played an important part in healing, perhaps in the diagnosis and prognosis of disease.

The entity gained through the activity, aiding in the temple service. When there were the various positions set in the Temple of Sacrifice, the entity was among the few that went through the whole course — or that occupied what today would be termed the seat of learning in the various twelve houses through which it was learned that the sun passed, that might apply to the individual in the material world.   3474-1

After individuals had completed their education in the Temple, they took "degrees" and were prepared for entering their position in society.

. . . the entity in its education was brought up in the school, as would be termed, in the Temple Beautiful; and along with the first ideas of vocational guidance or teachings that were a part of this institutional work, by the various groups that were designated through their choice or their abilities or their selection because of abilities . . . what later became known as the vocational help, or the groups that were educated by themselves, among themselves, was set as a part of that curriculum in the Temple Beautiful.

If these were to be changed from one environment to another, then they took degrees – as would be called today – through this station or channel – and were thus fortified or prepared for those changes that could or would be made from one group to another.   2533-4

Thus the various stations were established as to the form, the manner in which there was to be the preparation of individuals or groups for a *definite* service – whether as to motherhood, fatherhood, teachers, artisans, the artist, the legislator, the physician or the healer, or the instructors in all the various forms.   1472-10

Special counselors served in the Temple to help people in these choices.

The entity acted much in the capacity, as would be termed in the present, of one that was an analyzer of the abilities of others as related to their mental capacities, and mental abilities.   562-3

. . . the *entity* became then one that aided in the establishing of the *groups* that made for their choice in the portion of the expression to their fellow man.   982-4

The entity was among those who were chosen, because of the preparations of those with whom the entity became associated, to segregate those individuals into the fields chosen for their service in the material manifestations. Some were chosen to become strictly commercial, some were to adhere to what in the present is known as science; some were to be given to the arts; some to the studies as to the political influence, religious influence, home building, state building; and some were to prepare for services in other lands.

Then the entity was among those who were put at the head of the departments that were to choose these from the young and old, as you would term. Their preparations were made for same through the activities in the schools (you would call them such), or the Temples of Sacrifice and the Temple Beautiful as termed in those periods.   1583-1

Art

Under the dominating influence of the Temple Beautiful, the range of artistic expression broadened after the Reconstruction. Decorations in the Temple were now under the supervision of Isis.

The decorations in [the] Temple Beautiful became more elaborate. These, with the supervision of Isis (now), and with the spiritual influence of Iso, brought more and more attendance of that part of man's development.   294-152

67

Sculptors, working with various materials, began to idealize the human form.

> ... in the temple of recreation, where *now* only those that had gained that position where their bodies in form presented the human form divine, or the lines that were seen by the carvers in stone, the workers in brass, the moulders in iron, the wrought in gold of Ra ...   294-152

> ... the entity gained throughout — being active in the greater expression of the figures, the casts. For, the entity then cast the figures of the Priest's companion, as well as of the Young King, that became a part of that worshiped for its *beauty* — *not* for the character it represented! Please interpret aright the difference there! It interpreted the beauty as from the winged pharaoh, the goddess of love — not because it represents a portion of any experience but the beauty depicted by the character of the individual in the figure so made.   2537-1

The precepts taught in the Temple were rendered in symbolic images.

> The symbolized ideas in the homes, in the buildings, and the acceptance of this, that or the other that contributed to the welfare of man, found an individual that claimed — or set about to, in some form, add that to *their* contribution of man's development. Hence as the ibex, the scarab, the sacred ox, the sun, the eagle, and those in nature of every character that aided or abetted in representing an ideal of an individual brought into prominence by their ability to preserve same in some manner or form.
>   294-152

> The entity then made those plaques, and these will be found when the Temple of Records is opened; many of these where the signs, the symbols were given, were for the aiding of the individuals in holding before themselves that which would be helpful, aidful, in comprehending their relationship to the whole.   275-35

> Especially would be indicated the hawked figure or hawked god — the sacred oxen, also the scarab; with the figure of the oxen drawing the scow or plow.   1152-14

Lapidary crafts were extremely refined and used in decorating buildings.

> [The entity] then was in that particular phase of *adorning* the buildings especially with the gems or precious stones of that day ... the decorations in the temples, the homes, the associations in the activity during that particular experience and sojourn, were planned or advised with the entity then, in the name At-Lais.   955-1

> ... the entity rose to power, position, place, fame, through the experiences in that period, as related to the various manners of expression of praise in music, in art, and *especially* in that of placing of stones.   1719-1

The *arts,* in the broader sense; as workers in precious stones, silver, gold, and the more delicate metals that required the more intrinsic activity of individuals.   378-13

Artists specialized in color, painting, and woodworking.

. . . a painter of plaques, casts, and an enameler became the entity . . .
                                                                                            1918-1

. . . for the entity then that one who gave the greater to the designs of throne and of temple, in wood, and in the application of color, stain, dye . . .   39-2

Workers in fabrics, especially linen, designed styles of dress:

The entity then among those that were the keepers of the linens, and of those of the dress — or that as needed in the temple worship. Then, in this experience, the entity rather the one that made much fine linen, made much of the drawings that made for the vestry of the peoples in that period.   23-1

The entity then among those who were of the household of the King that invaded, and was the King's custodian of those of the buildings for the body, or as would be termed in the present the modiste, or tailor, for the royalty of that period.   1720-1

. . . then we find the establishing of the King's household; then we find begins the bodily adornment, and the first preparation for such was of the linens that have not as yet been attained in this particular period, since that as was set by those who *established* this linen development from the cottons, and the hemp, and the papyrus flowers and lotus flowers of this particular period.   294-151

As to the dress of the day, whether in the temple service or otherwise, this was always of linen — and in the manner as indicated, in the color as indicated, white and purple. The men and women were not much different in the manner of dress, save as in the Atlanteans who wore trousers when they came and coats, though much shorter or longer according to their class or distinction of their class. The king in his better moments was clad in the linens and the purples, and in the higher developments no change from the subjects at service.   275-38

Music

Music now permeated cultural life, with sounds and songs contributed by many different peoples.

The entity then, as El-ke-dun, was the first to combine the reeds and the lyre or the stringed instruments as a combination for the songs of the Atlanteans, the natives' chant, the wild revelry of its own land, to arouse the emotions necessary for concerted activity of the peoples.   1476-1

The entity was among the natives of that land and peoples who rose to activity and service in the Temple Beautiful for special activity as an emissary from the activities that brought music as well as verse and song, and the manners or means of giving expression to the emotions of the people of the period.   1921-1

The entity then among those who gave in the temple worship the song, the praise, and the ability of individuals to give rhythm and the harmony of voice and body.   4500-1

An orchestra in the Temple Beautiful created music to inspire spiritual attunement.

... and the entity was the leader then in what today would be termed the orchestra, or of those that made music for those as they swayed in body-movement — as in the chants that aided in the individual raising the thoughts in the praise of that power which impelled through *thinking* (as would be termed today), or the attuning of the spiritual selves to the attunement of the universal forces.   275-33

Instruments included harps, violas, reeds, and flutes:

Hence the entity became among the first users of the harp, or the lyre — as was later called, of the instrument. But in the entity's own periods there were rather the harps shaped as today, except they were much smaller and only carried then sixteen strings.   275-33

... those of the stringed instruments — as were played well by the entity — became a portion of the service re-established; a weaver and a musician ...   1918-1

Hence the instruments used were of the reed or flute, that is known in the present, and made the hearts of many merry; not as of those that would gratify the satisfying of carnal forces, but rather that as awakened within each those abilities for the expressing of — in its physical body — the music of the spirit in its activity in and through the body.   276-6

As noted (see pp. 24-25), chanting formed an important part of temple service. There were various chants for specific purposes:

... as the chant of the warrior, as the chant for the dead, as the chant for those that were being cleansed from impurities, as the chant for those who separated themselves for definite work.   1476-1

Religion

It is somewhat misleading to put the religion of that period into an exclusive category. This quest for spiritual understanding permeated every facet of Egyptian life and was the motivating center upon which the entire culture was focused.

There were, however, special services wherein the mystery of the Spirit was conveyed through ritual and symbol, and the temples contained places of activity which were especially sacred. The Priest "gave the entrance into the Holy of Holies ..." (341-9)

If it is not apparent from all the cultural forms mentioned so far, and if a distinction between "high" and "low" religion may be assumed, the readings make it clear that this was a period of "high" religion. In anthropological terms, we could say that it was an advanced form of monotheism.

The entity then assisted in giving much to these peoples the foundation of the truth of the relations of earthly individuals with the High God of the Heavens. The entity then in the name as called Araaraart.   341-8

. . . the entity was among those who led, being of the ruling force that combined again the forces of the King and the Priest; then acting in the capacity of the keeper of the temple as set aside by King *and* Priest for the worship of the Most High God.   2056-1

. . . men were taught to gain better understanding of the relationships of man to man, and of the Creative Energy-God to man, and man to God.
          5540-5

The religious tenets of this period became the foundation of the teachings of Christ, thousands of years later.

Then, in the activities of those, there arose much, many, and heaps of those same tenets as were given by Him Who first gave, "The meek shall inherit the earth."   254-42

. . . yet this sojourn in particular, and the activities of the entity, being the root or the beginning of that as became the tenet of the lessons given by Him who made Himself One with the Creative Energy in the earth's plane.   341-24

The spiritual services in the temples were oriented to the specific needs of each individual.

Q-8. Will you please give me that which was read in the hearing of those in the temple, who sought to know the way, sought to know the understanding of that that would be accomplished in their lives?

A-8. Each came with that, as has been termed later by some sects, as their confession, and as these needs were expressed or made known to the entity, that as was necessary for their awakening was seen, known, felt, by the entity. This may *best* be described as *feelings, rather* than words; for, as was said to many by the entity, as was said by the *Master* to some that would be healed, "Go wash in the pool, *then* present thyself to the priest according to the law thou hast been taught in." To another, "Thy sins be forgiven thee; take up thy bed, go into thine own house." To another, "No man, Lord." "Neither do I condemn thee, go and sin no more." The *needs,* as is necessary for the acts of individuals in the present, to lay down – or to put *off* a burden – may be felt by the entity, rather than being put into words; yet with the understanding does the entity know innately as to whether such an one is to read such and such prayer, is to wash in water to be clean, is to abstain from meats, or those of drug, or what not. Then, that seen is that as is felt as the message necessary for each individual who seeks in *His* name. 993-3

The following describes an entrance into the services of the Temple Beautiful:

Q-3. Give a description of the meeting with the priest, and the effect of the teachings upon the soul-mind.
A-3. This may be rather hard to put into words of the present day, for first was the meeting with the emissaries. Then there was the meeting with that activity in the temple, where there was sought the understanding within the spiritual-mindedness of the entity for cleansing — or preparation of self. And with the meeting of the priest, the aid as to the particular activity of the entity in those relations. The scene might be laid like this:

In the Temple Beautiful there was the music for the ones presenting themselves to be offered upon the altars for the cleansing of that which would prevent them from — what would be termed today — consecrating their lives to church through the baptismal service; though in that baptism it was by the altar first for the removing of those things that made for the carnal influence.

The entity then was among those who had been led in, or through the first experience of being offered on the altar and being presented by the priestess or the activity of that one in the temple so offering same made for the obeisance, as would be called, in pleading for the aid to assist self. It was robed in the garments of the Temple itself, in what later became the character of Egyptian robes of that particular period, made from the linens of the papyrus and the lotus combined and covered with the combination of the colors — purple and white — used as the robes of those so offering themselves. In such a scene was the meeting made.

As to the activities produced in the entity itself, there was rather the turn to the material abilities in controlling the animal force such as to present same in the music that aided in the worship or service in the Temple's activities later. 276-6

The robes of the priest would be blue-gray, with the hooded portion back from the head, while about the waist would be a cord of gold color, with a purple tassel — or one of the tassels — showing. The sandals would be of papyrus or woven grass. The robe of the kneeling figure would be in white (this also a robe, you see), with a band about the neck or throat in blue, not too dark, and the bare feet, or at least one or both showing.
585-10*

After the Reconstruction, Ra Ta formulated a code of ethics and issued laws through the temples.

In the matter of the temple, or the relationships of man to man, with the change in the home, with the change to the building up of the various

*Description for a life seal.

72

sections in or under their own rule, there became the necessity of establishing the rules and regulations that governed the relationships of individuals to individuals, as a criterion, as a measuring stick, as it were, as to what would be the ideal — or that that would be proper and right.   294-151

As cities developed in other parts of Egypt, the Temple Beautiful established centers in each community, staffed with trained counselors and teachers.

These were supervised by those that were close in association with the Priest; he, the Priest, then acting more and more in the capacity of the advisor, yet not those close in contact save with those that were active as emissaries in the various offices to which these were assigned as the developments began, not only in the place around Luz but also in those cities that were established in the various sections of the land.

As related to the spiritual life, with the establishing then of the home, of the various communities and the various towns and cities, there were also set those in the Temple Beautiful that acted in the capacity of advisors, teachers, ministers, or the ones giving counsel in the spiritual places that were prepared in the various centers.   294-151

Chapter Six

THE EVOLVING CULTURE

The Law of Evolution

Was Ra Ta's quest for the purification of the race in accord with the Law of Evolution, that law which the readings refer to as God's purpose? This was an important question which, it appears, did not receive adequate consideration in that period of family planning and physical purifications. The readings clearly state that Ra Ta was amiss in certain aspects of his desire for a "perfect" human form.

The boundary between right and wrong in Ra Ta's programs is very subtle; delicate racial questions arise in connection with his interpretation of Divine purpose. Certainly one can see the correctness of ridding individuals of animal appendages to free them for self-determination in mental and spiritual development. In addition, providing the means for achieving physical fitness or purification is in line with the readings' concept that the body is the "temple of the living God" and that a purified body enhances spiritual service.

It was when Ra Ta chose particular physical traits to represent an "ideal human form," and attempted to achieve this form as quickly as possible, that the readings find the Priest in error.

The traits which Ra Ta chose as divine were a symmetrical physique, *white skin, blonde hair and blue eyes.* Ra Ta himself had been one of the first in *that* period with white skin. (Note: The readings say that five races, among them the white, developed simultaneously when "entities" first came into the earth plane to occupy human form. We might speculate that by the time of this Egyptian period intermarriage had erased this racial demarcation.)

Ra Ta's daughter, Is-Is-Ao, inherited these rare physical characteristics, and the resultant prejudice brought turmoil into her life.

74

Remember, the entity's parent, Ra Ta, or Ra, was among the first of the men who had been purified to that of the whole or the *white*, see? This within itself brought to the entity disturbing forces, owing to its *own* condition in relationships to its alteration or change from the environs — or those about the entity being different.   1100-26

Hence, as Ra Ta means and indicates, among — or the first *pure* white in the experience then of the earth.   294-147

For, few of those had arisen to that state in which there were the preparations so as to produce the alabaster or all white . . .   2329-3

Initially, so few individuals had white skin that they were considered quite out of the ordinary.

The entity then was among those from the lands that were later called the Parthenian lands, or what ye know as the Persian land from which the conquerors then of Egypt had come.

As a Princess from that land the entity came to study the mysteries for the service it might give to those of her own land, the Carpathians — or as has been given, the entity was among the *first* of the pure white from that land to seek from the Priest and those activities in the Temple Beautiful for the purifying of self . . .   1472-1

Racial prejudice in this period involved not only skin color, but also appendages.

But those groups or individuals where there were racial prejudices, racial colors, racial activities (giving off the radiation such as to become odoriferous in certain characterizations, that become repulsive to something within individuals), these — as indicated in the entity's experience — were something to be conquered there.   585-12

One individual was "cured" of racial prejudice through Temple purifications involving electric therapy:

Then, to make application of same the entity found greater disturbances with the Atlantean peoples because of their color, because of their odor. These became very repulsive to the entity until — through those purifications in the Temple — there was the changing of those vibrations of the body forces through the electrical charges that were a part of the application that becomes a part of man's experience in the present . . . There, as may be experienced, when such are used in various forms, they may not only destroy disorders or diseases in a body but may also change entirely the attitude of an individual towards the entertaining of certain characteristics that are a part of the urges held to be at variance with certain characteristics in other individuals; unless these have passed through their normal development of associations.   585-12

This person later became an emissary to other regions, working to correct racial prejudice.

The entity chose the Carpathian and those areas where there were the aversions to certain groups of individuals that had other characteristics, as: The associations with the feet of the goat, with the hoofs of the horse, with those things that had been associated with such. 585-12

The following individual exemplified what Ra Ta considered the ideal body:

> The entity was free of such [appendages], and hence became one that indicated a position to be attained — not only in the environ of the land itself but in the Atlantean land as well as for the sojourners there — as the Princess of the Persian or Aryan land. 1472-10

These "desired" physical attributes could be acquired in a single lifetime. One individual's appearance was described as:

> . . . five feet four inches in height. Bronze when beginning in the service, the pure white when cleansed, in color. In the cleansing the conditions cleansed from body. Fair of hair, blue eyes, ever active in all its associations — as needs be for the activities in the experience. 275-38

This was accomplished through techniques of the Temple of Sacrifice previously described, and the use of certain stones.

> For the entity was among those who had the ability to change the color, change the activities, through the vibrations of stone as well as the odors, as were about the body. 1616-1

Apparently altering genetic structures also effected this transformation in succeeding generations.

> The entity . . . was that one first completed in that physical evolution, as to being the perfect body — as indicated through the activity of the parents in the Temples of Sacrifice and in the Temple Beautiful. Thus the entity then, Tar-Ello, was the first of the fair face who also had fair hair and blue eyes; this indicating to the Priest a completing of the purpose that had been the physical intent in those activities undertaken. 2390-7

The pinnacle of this purification program was realized later in one of Ra Ta's children.

> The entity then was the younger of the daughters of the High Priest, Ra Ta, as there were those periods when there had been the regeneration and the choices for channels for the new race.
> To the peoples of that period the entity presented what was called the *sine qua non* for that development; the highest as attained through that experience. 2459-1

A crucial problem was that although Ra Ta considered fair complexion, fair hair and blue eyes as being ideal, they were not necessarily God's ideal for everyone. Pushing physical development so rapidly may have prevented the conditions necessary for an individual's soul growth. This was even true for Ra Ta's own bodily regeneration.

For, the Priest had not interpreted in himself that even that being attempted was a matter of spiritual evolution. Thus, as many an individual, the Priest had attempted to hurry the process, or to placate God's purposes with individuals.

In this the Priest had also regenerated self, as to turn back time — as it were — in his own body. This, too, as will be seen in part, was not in keeping with the whole law of spiritual evolution.   2390-7

Many people in the Temples became tempted through Ra Ta's program to use spiritual disciplines for this purely material gain.

Many of the individuals who were associated with the Priest in the various offices, however, were tempted or taught — as it were — by the misinterpretation of the law by the Priest himself. For there was the attempt to placate the law of evolution. While these activities brought within themselves conditions that greatly improved the situations, they left in the mental self the applying of spiritual law to attain material desires — without the mental concepts being in accord.   2823-3

One who fell into this error of emphasizing the physical attributes and losing the spiritual import was Tar-Ello:

These were the periods that brought changes. The entity gave way to the material things, and self-indulgences brought in the latter portion of that period regrets — that, next to jealousy, sap the spiritual purpose in the mental attributes of body and mind of an individual manifested in materiality.   2390-7

The following was said of Ra Ta's daughter:

Yet the entity misused portions of that activity in such ways and manners as to cause a falling away from the mindfulness of preparations through the Temple of Sacrifice. For there was the tendency of the entity to overemphasize that activity in the Temple Beautiful, as to make it of little effect in the developing of those in the latter portion of that sojourn.
                                                                        2459-1

Ministry

As the Reconstruction transformed Egypt into a place of progress in every aspect of human existence, this land began to gain a reputation abroad.

. . . for with the regeneration, more and more became noised abroad that which had been and was being accomplished in this land of plenty, in foods, in ornaments, in the recreation, in the needs of the inner man, in the necessities for the satisfying of desires for the material mind, in the aiding or setting up of the various conditions that are called sciences in the present period.   294-151

Egypt sent out a world-wide invitation for all peoples to share its accomplishments.

> ... there was the invitation (as it might be called in the present) for those of *every* land to become acquainted with the activities of the King, the Priest, and those from the Atlantean land of that day ...   1472-10

The great teachers and wise men from the lands Ra Ta had visited began journeying to the Nile Valley to witness the advancements being made.

> These made for more and more visitations of the wise men, or the emissaries from the various lands, which heretofore had been visited by this priest Ra Ta.   294-151

The great teachers of the period were Ra Ta from Egypt, Saneid from India, Contui from Gobi, Tao from Mongolia, Yak from Carpathia, and Ajax from Atlantis.

> ... the entity was in that land now known as the Egyptian, during those periods when there were the attempts of many to make for the correlation of the thought between what had been developed in the Egyptian land with the return of the Priest, and the teachings in the Indian land of one Saneid, and the teachings in what was then the Mongoloid land or the Gobi Desert land — as known in the present — of one named Contui. 870-1

> ... with the establishing of the tenets that were as a united influence in the experience of the then known world, the entity became one who carried to those of many lands the correlating influence from those teachers; as Ra Ta in Egypt, Ajax the teacher from Atlantis, Saneid from India, Yak [?] from Carpathia, Tao from Mongolia. The teachings of these were combined ...   991-1

Certain aspects of the Atlantean religious practices are especially interesting.

> ... the entity was in that now known as or called the Egyptian land, during those periods when there were those journeying hither from the Atlantean land.

> The entity then was the princess of fire, or that one of the Law of One who acted in the capacity oft of the interpreter from and to the masters, the sons of the Most High, that would communicate with those in the earth.

> Then the entity, as Princess Ilax, made for the establishing of the material activities in the sun god worship, that were later set up by Isis, Ra, Hermes, Ra Ta and those who became the teachers ...   966-1

Teachings were gathered from as far away as the Americas:

> ... when there were the settlements and the Priest had become again active in giving the service or principles to not only the natives but in assisting to bring a greater understanding to all the nations roundabout; when there had been the call for the activities from the teachings of

78

Saneid, from the Pyrenees, from the Mongoloid, from what is now known as Indo-China, the Inca, those peoples that were left of the Atlanteans, the Yucatan, and what is now the American land. 1438-1

. . . the entity was in the land now known as the Egyptian, during those periods when there were the re-establishings after the return of the Priest to the land; when there were the beginnings of the correlating of the tenets from Mongolia, Caucasia, India, Oz and Mu — or that now known as the American land, or the Zu of the Oz. 980-1

As this eclectic compendium of knowledge was being gathered in Egypt a great correlation of truths began. All the religious practices and spiritual perspectives of the time were first classified and then synthesized in an attempt at a universal understanding of a Higher Being.

There [in Egypt] the entity made for the greater progress in its development from the mental or soul experiences, in that particular period. For with the return of the Priest, with the gatherings of the various understandings or teachings, the entity then made a study of such; and classified and interpreted same for the many, so that *application* of same might be made in the experiences of those in the Egyptian land as well as in the Indian, the Mongoloid or Mongolian or Gobi, the Carpathian, and the Og, and those lands across the seas in those experiences. 1135-1

Then the entity made the relationships with those in foreign lands that there might be the exchange of ideas, the exchange of the activities to which there might be a correlation of same with the establishings of those tenets in that experience. 695-1

The knowledge which had been gathered was stored in what could be called libraries:

. . . the entity became the keeper of that put in the treasure house for the dispersing *of* that knowledge in *foreign* fields, home fields, in the building *up* of the temple, in the building up of the King's household . . . 1925-1

This international combination of philosophies and teachings was translated into the laws and tenets of the land.

And the abilities of the entity were used in helping to correlate the teachings of Ra Ta with the teachings of Ajax and Saneid and the activities in the various lands . . . in establishing what would become not only the moral law but the penal law, and the spiritual law in relation to man in his various changes being made . . . 1007-1

. . . we find [the entity] in the land known as the Egyptian, during that period when there were divisions in the land, when there were . . . the establishing of the relationships of penal law, material law, martial law, religious law, as compared to the experiences of the sages, or of the lands far and near. 1720-1

With Egypt as its center, a world-wide ministry was set in motion. Emissaries traveled throughout the world, disseminating those truths which had as their common denominator the Law of One. Some went to India:

> And when there was the re-establishing, and the building, and the beginning of the activity that made for the sending out of those that were to be teachers, ministers, aids in helping others, the entity may be said to have builded, to have dedicated in the Indian land, the first of the sacred fires in Delhi as now known — then Deoi. 812-1

Others went to Italy and France:

> . . . the activities, those things that had been set in force by the entity itself — in the name Heb-hen — made for the aid to many of the lands to which those tenets, those lessons, were carried. Hence those peoples in what is now the Italian land, the French land, were supplied with the first of the spiritual purposes by the activities of this entity making those overtures in that direction. 695-1

Mongolia:

> The entity remained true throughout that period, becoming close companion to the entity or Priest, raised to the position of interpreter to those who came from foreign lands, to those who were sent as emissaries to gather the news of that as gained. The entity then went as the representative, in the latter days, passing from the stage of activity in the far land known now as the Mongolian. 1924-1

Travels to Abyssinia, Persia, Gobi, Greece and the Americas are mentioned in subsequent readings.

Many in Egypt gave up their vocations to answer the call for foreign ministry. Councilors became emissaries:

> The entity was among the twelve councilors, then, during that period of activity. Later, with the establishing of the relationships with the Atlanteans and the various groups from other lands, the entity was the emissary. 289-9

Atlanteans became emissaries:

> . . . the entity was in the Atlantean land, when there were those periods of preparation for leaving the land; through the teachings of the Law of One, of which the entity was a member — and not only a member but a princess in same . . .
>
> When the divisions came the entity was among those who went into the Egyptian land; first in the Pyrenees land, then — with the acceptance of the Priest of Egypt and the King, and the attempts for the correlation of these for applications in the experiences of those of the land — the entity, as Mayr, made for great help to the peoples from the Abyssinian land and the peoples from the Indian land — or from Saneid and the peoples from the land of Mu and the Golden City, or City of Gold.

Hence the entity as an emissary, as a teacher in those periods, aided much in the establishing of the unity of purposes through the various centers.   1592-1

The Priest's grandson became an emissary:

... the entity was in the Egyptian land, among those in the household of the Priest — being a grandson of the Priest, and a son of one of the daughters of the Priest by his first wife.

This brought the opportunity for the use of the entity's abilities in those activities during the development of those periods when the emissaries and representatives were being prepared for the many lands.

The entity then acted in the capacity of heading the various groups that were sent as representatives, as missionaries or emissaries, not only as a political and economic influence but for the preservation of those activities in the relationships with others.   2294-1

Even the royal tailor became an emissary:

The entity then among those who were of the household of the King that invaded, and was the King's custodian of those of the buildings for the body, or as would be termed in the present the modiste, or tailor, for the royalty of that period. Gaining through the experience through the ministry as given, also as to the conditions that the entity served under during that experience; becoming of those that were ambassadors later to other lands, and the entity among those in the land who went as an emissary to what is now America.   1720-1

Reporters covered the progress being made in the various lands.

... the entity was in that now known as or called the Egyptian experience, when there were the disseminations of the truths that had been and were being correlated by the teachers of many lands; in the first seminaries, in the diffusion of the powers and forces of men and women.

The entity then, in the name Ileano, made for the greater advancement in its *earthly* experience, through the dissemination of those tenets that the Priest and those of that period had given and did give to many peoples.

Then the entity was what would today be termed a reporter of many activities in many lands; going to those people in Abyssinia, Persia, India, Mongolia, Carpathia, Portugal, and Atlantis just before the destruction.
                                                                                                                                954-1

In certain places emissaries set up new centers, which in turn gathered knowledge from many foreign sources. These centers often became cultural nuclei in themselves, and they lasted for thousands of years.

The entity then was among the leaders and emissaries, and was an emissary to the Carpathian land; being of those peoples from the Atlantean land. And with the training and the tenets of the Law of One, those things pertaining to that which first brought the conveniences in the lives of those that were home builders, and then those things that made for the establishing and acknowledging of the relationships of the individuals to their fellow man and to the Creative Forces — the entity established same in that land which later from its teachings founded what is known as the Grecian regime.

In the experience the entity gained, in the name Ax-Ten-Tel.   1150-1

The entity made for the gatherings of these as groups from the various centers, that made for the setting up of an independent activity by the entity in what is now the Persian and Arabian land; gathering influences and forces not only from the Egyptian land but the Indian, the Mongolian, the Gobi, and also from the Caucasian or the northern lands of what is now Norway, Denmark and the Teutonic land. For the entity then became a great leader during that experience, in the name Barrai.   870-1

. . . we find [the entity] in that sojourn in the land now known as Egypt, during those experiences when many were being taught in the ways of those peoples that had gathered there, and the Priest and his aides were sending out the emissaries to the varied lands.

The entity was among the princesses of India that came to that land of Ra, there gaining much in the activities with those in the temples of service, as to how the bodies might be purged from the wayward forces and influences in their experience. In the Temple of Sacrifice and in the Temple Beautiful did the entity gain . . .

Then in the name Susi-set, the entity went again to her own lands, and began to give to her *own* peoples in that land what had been gained in the experiences in Egypt. And there was kept for the whole period of the entity's sojourn those relations with those that aided in adding to the young peoples in that land the lessons of life as applied to the material body, and in giving out their influence to others.   497-1

And with the correlating of the thought, the entity became first as the representative of the Temple Beautiful in the Indian land; and later — and during the period of its greatest height — in the land of the Gobi, or the Mongoloid. *There* the entity was as the Priestess in the Temple of Gold, which is still intact there.

The entity then, as Shu-shent, made for great development . . .   987-2

The entity then was among those in what is now the desert land, and in the city of Nu [?] — Enu [?] — being the queen of that particular city, making for the self that of a kingdom within a kingdom from the material standpoint. During the sojourn took for self and her own peoples not only the tenets of the Priest but of the Nubians, the Atlanteans, the Indians, and also of that land from which the people came who were in rule then in the Egyptian land. And the entity used these in the activities in her own kingdom or sojourn. Hence there may be seen today, even in the upper coast of that land along the great sea, that there are those who claim to be descendants of a mighty and powerful goddess that brought to her people a new understanding.   757-8

The teachings of these were combined, and the *entity* was the leader in carrying the forces that ministered — as it were, in making the *bodily* coordinating influences in the teachings; so that there were the *united* efforts in the buildings in what became Bethel. And in that land did the entity then make for that indeed as Bethel means, "Silence is golden, if thou art in the presence of God." 991-1

Of course, this massive undertaking required a tremendous supervisory staff in Egypt. Henk-elel was in charge of foreign relations at home.

... the entity was in the Egyptian land when there had been the setting up of an ideal by the Priest and especially by the King who had chosen the councilors for providing a better understanding between peoples of other lands and setting, as would be called in the present, the offices for the aid — or the Cabinet of the President. Then the entity was President of the young King . . . In all the various portions and forms of that set as tenets and teachings, the entity . . . represented the King and the Priest in his efforts with other groups — as those in the Carpathian, the Persian, the land of Saad, the Golden Land and especially in the Gobi land. 5395-1

... the entity was in the name Arar-apth . . . and among those specifically that headed the distribution of the tenets that were lastly set in building up the spiritual truths for the material activities of the peoples in the land — and to those lands to whom emissaries were sent. 478-1

Then the entity [Len-Loiden] was one in power as to those things partaking of the social and moral and religious relationships of individuals and groups for active services in either of the Temples; and to those did the entity counsel much that became emissaries and missionaries in the various teachings and relationships to many another land. 1346-1

Through this ministry, Ra Ta — in 10,500 B.C. — influenced world history from that time on.

The Library of Alexandria

The Library of Alexandria was founded during this period. Its fame and importance, especially that of its classical period, is legendary.

The library was first established by Apex-el, an Atlantean who sailed to the Pyrenees in Spain and France and later came to Egypt.

The entity was among those that set sail for the Egyptian land, but entered rather into the Pyrenees and what is now the Portuguese, French and Spanish land. And there *still* may be seen in the chalk cliffs there in Calais the activities, where the marks of the entity's followers were made, as the attempts were set with those to create a temple activity to the follower of the Law of One.

Then in the name Apex-el, the entity lost and gained. Lost during those periods when there were the turmoils and strife that brought about the necessity for the sojourning from the land and the entering into the others.

Gained when there was the establishing of the associations with those that had built up the Egyptian land. And, as will be seen from those that may yet be found about Alexandria, the entity may be said to have been the first to begin the establishment of the library of knowledge in Alexandria; ten thousand three hundred before the Prince of Peace entered Egypt for His first initiation there. For, read ye, "He was crucified also in Egypt." 315-5

The library was one of the greatest repositories of knowledge in all history. When emissaries began to travel to various regions, they conveyed knowledge based on research at the Library of Alexandria.

The entity then among those, or that *one* given charge of that land then known as Deoshe [?] — now Alexandria — that founded that making for the greatest collection of manuscripts, of writings, of the various forces, that has ever been known in the *world* of experience in the earth's plane. The *entity* then the *founder* of that as carried on by successive generations of the entity's descendants, as Ariecel. In this experience the entity gained much through those associations of the ruler and of those that acted with the peoples that became emissaries; for as this was the outlet to many portions of the country to which emissaries and ambassadors were sent, the entity acted in the capacity of the one making the exchange and supplying those forces that builded for relationships with groups and individuals. 412-5

One of Ra Ta's daughters was among those who worked to establish the library.

The entity then was an associate or companion of the Priest's daughter; not as one of the opposite sex, but rather as the best friend or associate in the beginning of the activities for establishing a center of culture in what is now Alexandria, that began the collection of data, books, records of various groups. 2835-1

The principality of the Ibex also assisted the cultural development of Alexandria.

. . . the entity was in that land known as the Egyptian, among those people that separated themselves during the rebellious forces, and among those peoples of Ibex that later made for the establishing of those foundations of a teaching in what later became known as Alexandria . . . the peoples there, or the temples there. 603-1

The Library of Alexandria contained knowledge from many countries:

. . . the concepts and the relationships innately and manifestly that become a part of the entity's *soul*-mind development, and the mental or physical-mind development as may be applied in the present [became a part of the entity's study]; from the information obtained or contacts made, especially in the studies made by the entity in the great library that was a part of the entity's experience during the sojourn in what is now known as Alexandria — where there had been the gatherings of data from or by the sages of old. For all of those influences and forces of not only the Egyptians and the Persians and the lands beyond the seas, but the activities in the many other lands, were included in the records there.

877-27

Thousands of years later, travelers from Judea — including Josie and Mary (mother of Jesus) — came to Alexandria and studied in the library.

Do not understand that there was only Joseph, Mary, Josie and the Child. For there were other groups that preceded and followed; that there might be the physical protection to that as had been considered by these groups of peoples as the fulfilling of the Promised One.

In the journeys to Egypt, little of great significance might be indicated, but the care and attention to the Child and the Mother was greatly in the hands of this entity, Josie, through that journey.

The period of sojourn in Egypt was in and about, or close to, what was then Alexandria.

Josie and Mary were not idle during that period of sojourn, but those records — that had been a part of those activities preserved in portions of the libraries there — were a part of the work that had been designated for this entity. And the interest in same was reported to the Brotherhood in the Judean country.

1010-17

When Jesus had reached maturity, he went to Egypt for instruction at an Essene school in Heliopolis. Records of this visit were stored in Alexandria, but were lost in the destruction of this great library.

Q-13. Please describe Jesus' education in Egypt in Essene schools of Alexandria and Heliopolis, naming some of His outstanding teachers and subjects studied.

A-13. Not in Alexandria — rather in Heliopolis, for the periods of attaining to the priesthood, or the taking of the examinations there — as did John. One was in one class, one in the other . . .

Q-16. Why does not the Bible tell of Jesus' education, or are there manuscripts now on earth that will give these missing details to be found soon?

A-16. There are some that have been forged manuscripts. All of those that existed were destroyed — that is, the originals — with the activities in Alexandria.

2067-7

Chapter Seven

THE HERITAGE

A positive nationalism developed – a spirit of *e pluribus unum.*

Then began what may be truly termed the first national or nation *spirit* of a peoples; for with the divisions, rather than this causing a dispersing of ideals or a dividing up of interests, it *centralized* the interests . . .
294-151

Ra Ta, now known as Ra, was

. . . preparing for this very spirit to manifest itself in the way of the national emblems, the national ideas, that stood for the varied activities of not only individuals or groups, but for the general masses.   294-151

Ra therefore conceived one of history's most significant "emblems."

THE GREAT PYRAMID

Hence there began the first preparation for what has later become that called The Great Pyramid . . .   294-151

Hermes, a cryptic figure in the readings, became the construction architect of the Great Pyramid, commissioned by Araaraart. Isis acted as an advisor.

. . . the entering in of Hermes *with* Ra – who came as one of the peoples from the mount to which these peoples had been banished . . . Hence under the authority of Ra, and Hermes as the guide, or the actual (as would be termed in the present) constructing or construction architect with the Priest or Ra giving the directions – and those of Isis (now) in the form of the advisor . . .   294-151

The Pyramid was to be a monumental repository of knowledge and prophecy, and also serve as the Temple of Initiation for the White Brotherhood.

Then, with Hermes and Ra (those that assumed or took up the work of Araaraart) there began the building of that now called Gizeh, with which those prophecies that had been in the Temple of Records and the Temple Beautiful were builded, in the building of this that was to be the Hall of the Initiates of that sometimes referred to as the White Brotherhood.   5748-5

The building was begun with Atlantean assistance:

For there was not only the adding to the monuments, but the Atlanteans aided in their activities with the creating of that called the Pyramid, with its records of events of the earth through its activity in all of the ages to that in which the new dispensation is to come.   281-43

Hept-Supht acted as a supervisor:

. . . aiding in the re-establishing of the Temple Beautiful, the Temple of Records, and the beginnings of the distribution of the tenets or aids as they were given out to others – in the name Hept-Supht.

In the experience the entity gained, for he was among those that later became the supervisors in the building of the Pyramid that is the mystery as yet – today.   378-12

Ajax-ol, the Atlantean scientist who had developed the use of electricity, now applied his abilities to the task of incorporating prophecy into the design of the Pyramid:

. . . the rise and fall of the nations were to be depicted in this same temple that was to act as an interpreter for that which had been, that which is, and that which is to be, in the material plane.   294-151

This, then, receives all the records from the beginnings of that given by the Priest, Arart, Araaraart and Ra, to that period when there is to be the change in the earth's position and the return of the Great Initiate to that and other lands for the folding up of those prophecies that are depicted there. All changes that came in the religious thought in the world are shown there, in the variations in which the passage through same is reached, from the base to the top – or to the open tomb *and* the top. These are signified by both the layer and the color in what direction the turn is made.   5748-5

These colors, that presented or represented the various periods, as well as the interpretations of On [?], Ra Ta and Hermes, and the wise men of the period, were placed by the orders of the entity then – as Ajax-ol.
2462-2

Oelom, the former revolutionary, assisted in the interpretation of the historical data to be incorporated.

Q-1. What connection did the entity have at that time with the building of The Great Pyramid?

A-1. A great deal in various experiences of same; that is, in the interpreting of periods of those activities which preceded that period in which the building was begun there. For, remember, this was not an interpretation only from that period *forward*, but as to the very *place* and experience in which there is to be the change in the activities in the earth!

849-45

As opposed to the popular belief, the construction of the Great Pyramid did not necessarily involve thousands of workers dragging huge blocks of stone up an inclined plane.

Q-14. How was this particular Great Pyramid of Gizeh built?
A-14. By the use of those forces in nature as make for iron to swim. Stone floats in the air in the same manner. This will be discovered in '58.

5748-6

Q-3. By what power or powers were these early pyramids and temples constructed?
A-3. By the lifting forces of those gases that are being used gradually in the present civilization, and by the fine work or activities of those versed in that pertaining to the source from which all power comes. 5750-1

Even with these methods, the Pyramid took a hundred years to complete.

Q-5. What was the date of the actual beginning and ending of the construction of the Great Pyramid?

A-5. Was one hundred years in construction. Begun and completed in the period of Araaraart's time, with Hermes and Ra.

Q-6. What was the date B.C. of that period?
A-6. 10, 490 to 10, 390 before the Prince entered into Egypt. 5748-6

This building, as we find, lasted for a period of what is termed now as one hundred years. 294-151

The scientific and mathematical knowledge of that period was also incorporated into the Pyramid's design.

The entity was then among the *builders* of the period. And there were disputes that arose through those periods of activities, as to what pertained to or was in keeping with the astrological aspects, the numerological aspects, and those things that would be the more lasting in their relationships to the climatic conditions, the atmospheric pressures and the various influences had upon those temples and those monoliths. For it was during those periods that the laying out of some of the pyramids was begun, and also there were the explorations into the archaeological experiences.

1011-1

[The Great Pyramid] was to be the presentation of that which had been gained by these peoples through the activities of Ra Ta, who *now* was known as Ra . . . [and] there was brought the idea of the preservation of these, not only for those in the present but for the generations that were to come in the experiences and experiences throughout that period, until the changes were to come again in the earth's position . . . It was formed according to that which had been worked out by Ra Ta in the mount as related to the position of the various stars, that acted in the place about which this particular solar system circles in its activity, going towards what? That same name as to which the Priest was banished — the constellation of Libra, or to Libya were these people sent.   294-151

An individual named Pa-Rizla was among the first to devise methods of incorporating prophecy into architectural structures by the use of geometric relationships.

. . . the entity then builded the *first* of the pyramids that are yet not uncovered, and gave to the peoples that first concept of the square, the compass, and its meaning to those peoples as a mode of leaving for those that would study same, *history* in its making, history as has been builded. In a portion of that builded may there still be seen those of the activities *of* the entity, then in the name Pa-Rizla.   2124-3

The location of the Great Pyramid was determined with the utmost accuracy so that its very position would manifest geodetic and astronomical relationships.

When the lines about the earth are considered from the mathematical precisions, it will be found that the center is nigh unto where the Great Pyramid, which was begun then, is still located.   281-42

At the correct time accurate imaginary lines can be drawn from the opening of the Great Pyramid to the second star in the Great Dipper, called Polaris or the North Star. This indicates it is the system toward which the soul takes its flight after having completed its sojourn through this solar system.   5748-6

As a prophetic record, the Pyramid contains representations of specific events of the 20th Century, such as the Depression and World War II.

Q-4. *What are the correct interpretations of the indications in the Great Pyramid regarding the time when the present depression will end?*
A-4. The changes as indicated and outlined are for the latter part of the present year [1932]. As far as depression is concerned, this is not — as in the minds of many — because fear has arisen, but rather that, when fear has arisen in the hearts of the created, *sin* lieth at the door. Then, the change will occur — or that seeking will make the definite change — in the latter portion of the present year. Not that times financially will be better, but the minds of the people will be fitted to the conditions better . . .

Q-10. *What will be the type and extent of the upheaval in '36?*
A-10. The wars, the upheavals in the interior of the earth, and the shifting of same by the differentiation in the axis as respecting the positions from the Polaris center.   5748-6

Calculations were set in the Pyramid showing that a large number of Atlanteans and Lemurians would incarnate during this century.

In October [1932] there will be seen the first variation in the position of the polar star in relation to the lines from the Great Pyramid. The Dipper is gradually changing, and when this change becomes noticeable — as might be calculated from the Pyramid — there will be the beginning of the change in the races. There will come a greater influx of souls from the Atlantean, Lemurian, La, Ur or Da civilizations. These conditions are indicated in this turn in the journey through the Pyramid.   5748-6

According to the readings, this influx of souls signifies the beginning of a new "sub-race."

In those conditions that are signified in the way through the Pyramid, as of periods through which the world has passed and is passing, as related to the religious or the spiritual experiences of man — the period of the present is represented by the low passage or depression showing a downward tendency, as indicated by the variations in the character of stone used. This might be termed in the present as the Cruciatarian Age [?], or that in which preparations are being made for the beginning of a new sub-race, or a change, which — as indicated from the astronomical or numerical conditions — dates from the latter portion or middle portion of the present fall [1932]. In October there will be a period in which the benevolent influences of Jupiter and Uranus will be stronger, which — from an astrological viewpoint — will bring a greater interest in occult or mystic influences.   5748-6

The King's Chamber, with its empty sarcophagus, was designed to carry a profound symbolic message for the 20th Century.

Q-7. What definite details are indicated as to what will happen after we enter the period of the King's Chamber?
A-7. When the bridegroom is at hand, all do rejoice. When we enter that understanding of being in the King's presence, with that of the mental seeking, the joy, the buoyancy, the new understanding, the new life, through the period.

Q-8. What is the significance of the empty sarcophagus?
A-8. That there will be no more death. Don't misunderstand or misinterpret! but the interpretation of death will be made plain . . .

Q-12. What is the date, as recorded by the Pyramid, of entering in the King's Chamber?
A-12. '38 to '58   5748-6

The entity saw what was preserved as the memorials, the pyramids built during the entity's sojourn; when there was begun the Pyramid of understanding, or Gizeh — and only to the King's Chamber was the pathway built. But the entity will see in the present the empty tomb period pass; hence rise to heights of activity in the present experience.   275-33

90

The following extract illustrates the extreme accuracy of the Pyramid's record of prophecy:

Q-1. Are the deductions and conclusions arrived at by D. Davidson and H. Aldersmith in their book on The Great Pyramid correct?

A-1. Many of these that have been taken as deductions are correct. Many are far overdrawn. Only an initiate may understand.

Q-2. What corrections for the period of the 20th Century?

A-2. Only those that there will be an upheaval in '36.

Q-3. Do you mean there will be an upheaval in '36 as recorded in the Pyramid?

A-3. As recorded in the Pyramid, though this is set for a correction which, as has been given, is between '32 *and* '38 — the correction would be, for this — as seen — is '36 — for it is in many — these run from specific days; for, as has been seen, there are periods when even the hour, day, year, place, country, nation, town, and individuals are pointed out. That's how correct are many of those prophecies as made.   5748-5

The readings suggest that part of the prophetic record was destroyed during the later Egyptian dynasties.

In the period that is to come, this ends — as to that point which is between what is termed in chronological time in present — between 1950 and 1958, but there have been portions that have been removed by those that desecrated many of those other records in the same land. This was rejected by that Pharaoh who hindered in the peoples leaving the land.

5748-5

Q-9. If the Armageddon is foretold in the Great Pyramid, please give a description of it and the date of its beginning and ending.

A-9. Not in what is left there. It will be as a thousand years, with the fighting in the air, and — as has been — between those returning to and those leaving the earth.   5748-6

In the Ra Ta period, these chambers received the initiates who had graduated from the Temple Beautiful.

The entity was in the midst of these, as the companion of the builder of the pyramids, and as a director in same; or of that especial pyramid that was built not as a tomb but as a house of those who were dedicated to a special service. This was rather the house, or the way in which those who were edified were to receive their benediction, not only from the priests of the period but from the powers on high — as represented not only in the chambers but through the manners in which the history or the events of the times were put there. The entity then was a student of same.

2823-1

The last initiate to take His degrees in the Great Pyramid, some 10,000 years later, was the greatest of them all.

In this same Pyramid did the Great Initiate, the Master, take those last of the Brotherhood degrees with John, the forerunner of Him, at that place. As is indicated in that period where the entrance is shown to be in that land that was set apart, as that promised to that peculiar peoples, as were rejected — as is shown in that portion when there is the turning back from the raising up of Xerxes as the deliverer from an unknown tongue or land, and again is there seen that this occurs in the entrance of the Messiah in this period — 1998.   5748-5

Q-30. Please describe Jesus' initiations in Egypt, telling if the Gospel reference to "three days and nights in the grave or tomb," possibly in the shape of a cross, indicate a special initiation.

A-30. This is a portion of the initiation — it is a part of the passage through that to which each soul is to attain in its development, as has the world through each period of their incarnation in the earth. As is supposed, the record of the earth through the passage through the tomb, or the Pyramid, is that through which each entity, each soul, as an initiate must pass for the attaining to the releasing of same — as indicated by the empty tomb, which has *never* been filled, see? Only Jesus was able to break same, as it became that which indicated His fulfillment.   2067-7

Only those who have been called may truly understand. Who then has been called? Whosoever will make himself a channel may be raised to that of a blessing that is all that entity-body is able to comprehend. Who, having his whole measure full, would desire more does so to his own undoing.   5748-6

THE SPHINX

As the Great Pyramid was rising on the Giza Plateau, another monumental archetype was being prepared. At the eastern base of the Plateau, facing the rising sun, the enigmatic Sphinx still appears as a sentinel for the Temple of Initiation.

The Sphinx was founded upon ruins discovered during the archaeological activities of the Ra Ta period; it had existed as a monument even before the entrance of Arart into Egypt. Now it was being restored and transformed for specific symbolic import.

This work was actually begun before the banishment but completed in later years.

In the information as respecting the pyramids, their purpose in the experience of the peoples, in the period when there was the rebuilding of the Priest during the return in the land, some 10,500 before the coming of the Christ into the land, there was first that attempt to restore and add to that which had been begun on what is called the Sphinx, and the treasure or storehouse facing same, between this and the Nile, in which those records were kept by Arart and Araaraart in the period.   5748-5

With the return of the Priest (as it had been stopped), this was later — by Isis, the queen, or the daughter of Ra — turned so as to present to those peoples in that land the relationships of man and the animal or carnal world with those changes that fade or fall away in their various effect.

5748-6

Arsrha, a member of Arart's original invading tribe, supervised the building of the Sphinx.

He arranged then for the first monuments that were being restored and builded in those places, being then the founder of now that mystery of mysteries, the Sphinx . . .

Q-6. In what capacity did this entity act regarding the building of the Sphinx?

A-6. As the monuments were being rebuilt in the plains of that now called the pyramid of Gizeh, this entity builded, laid, the foundations; that is, superintended same, figured out the geometrical position of same in relation to those buildings as were put up of that connecting the Sphinx. And the data concerning same may be found in the vaults in the base of the Sphinx. We see this Sphinx was builded as this:

The excavations were made for same in the plains above where the temple of Isis [?] had stood during the deluge, occurring some centuries before, when this people (and this entity among them) came in from the north country and took possession of the rule of this country, setting up the first dynasty. The entity was with that dynasty, also in the second dynasty of Araaraart, when those buildings were begun. The base of the Sphinx was laid out in channels, and in the corner facing the Gizeh may be found the wording of how this was founded, giving the history of the first invading ruler and the ascension of Araaraart to that position. 195-14

The face of the Sphinx was formed to represent Asriaio, the Chief Councilor to Araaraart.

During this period was the completion of the memorial standing as the mystery of the ages today, and this, as is seen, represents this councilor to the kings, for, as is seen in the figure itself, not as one of the kings made in beast form, yet overseeing, supervising, giving council, giving strength, to the kings before and the kings since. The face, even as was given then, is the representation of this councilor to this great people.   953-24

The most important function of the Sphinx, however, was to guard the Temple of Records.

THE RECORDS

The entity aided in those activities, being among the children of the Law of One from Atlantis; *aiding* the Priest in that preparation, in that manner of building the temples of records that lie just beyond that enigma that still is the mystery of mysteries to those who seek to know what were the manners of thought of the ancient sons who made man — a beast — as a part of the consciousness.   2402-2

The monuments as were unearthed and added to from time to time, we find some still existent, though many buried beneath shifting sands. Others underneath sands that became the bed of the seas that overflowed this country.   341-9

What lies buried beneath the sands of the Giza Plateau? The readings suggest that archaeological exploration will eventually uncover a whole complex of channels, chambers, tombs and temples — bringing the Ra Ta period into contemporary consciousness.

As noted, when the Sphinx was built there were "those buildings as were put up of that connecting the Sphinx," and the base "was laid out in channels." Another reading specifies that the history of the Ra Ta period will be found "Not in the underground *channel* (as was opened by the ruler many years, centuries, later), but in the real base, or that as would be termed in the present parlance as the cornerstone." (953-24) We are also told that "there is a chamber or passage from the right forepaw to this entrance of the record chamber, or record tomb." (5748-6)

There are evidently several record chambers, for the readings often speak of them in the plural.

. . . these were to be kept as had been given by the priests in Atlantis or Poseidia (Temple), when these records of the race of the developments of the laws pertaining to One were put in their chambers . . .   378-16

The readings also indicate that, beneath the sand at Giza, there is more than one pyramid buried somewhere between the Sphinx and the Nile.

. . . the entity then builded the *first* of the pyramids that are yet not uncovered . . .

Q-1. In referring to the uncovered pyramids in the Egyptian land, near what present place are those pyramids?
A-1. Between that as is known as the Mystery of the Ages and the river.
2124-3

. . . for the later pyramids, or those yet not uncovered, that has been spoken of, are *between* the Sphinx (or the Mystery) *and* the Nile, or the river . . .   993-3

These pyramids contain storehouses which, in the Ra Ta period, housed gold and precious stones.

. . . and there may be found still those of the storehouse of El-Dhli, those storehouses in those pyramids or mounds not yet uncovered; for the entity became an *individual* of power through the great storehouse of gold, precious stones, and of those of worth both as those that had to do with *bodily* conditions as well as exchange among the peoples.   1925-1

We are told of temples that are to be discovered. This reading may or may not be another reference to the hidden pyramids:

> Many are the temples builded later in the plains that are yet to be uncovered, near the Sphinx, as seen at present, which represents a portion of contemporary forces and contemporaries during the period, see?   900-275

Artifacts

Many items common in the daily lives of those early Egyptians were put into the vaults. These included records of the schools, gold pieces, linen, and Araaraart's personal belongings.

> The entity in the name Isoda, and there still may be found among those of the entity's doings – among the records as made and kept through the establishing of the school, or Islo as called then in that period, that were placed among the effects of Araaraart in the mount not *yet* uncovered.
>
> 759-1

> The entity's influences may be seen in many of those findings as may be found in the pyramid [not] yet uncovered, for with the waiting on the Priest, with the ability of the active agent between the King and the teacher and the minister to the ill, the entity wrought in gold and in fine linen, many of those replicas of the day that may be found, *yet,* among those of the King's belongings, as well as of many of those that were placed therein.
>
> 69-1

> There the entity aided in the building, and in the preserving of records that will some day be a part of *some* men's physical or material consciousness. For these, as some of the lost arts – as the tempering of brass, as the manners in which there were the chemical weavings of the papyrus, as well as the preserving of those things necessary for the making of linens – all were a part of the entity's awareness and activities through those experiences there.   2246-1

The Record Chambers also contain musical instruments and compositions:

> *Q-10. Were there any musical instruments sealed in that room?*
> A-10. Many; not only those used in the Temple Beautiful in the temple service but those that aided in the service for those that danced, in their show of service in the temple. These, that were used then: The lyre, the harp, the flute, the viola.   378-16

> [The entity was] the musician in the temple after the restoration, and one that may yet be found many of even the *compositions* by the entity during that period, when that of the first of the pyramids is opened. 295-1

The entity served well during this experience, and in the same tombs of

those considered the great may the entity's tenets, the entity's gatherings
of precious stones and of the cymbals for the calling of the peoples to the
portion of the worship as presented by the entity, these may still be
found — and they are of a *peculiar* make, being in the form of the beetle
that was *later* worshiped by many for the beauty of the music that was
made in the use of same.   1923-1

The Record Chambers also contain dietary information and
medicinal compounds.

The entity's harps — and the entity's *menus,* as they would be termed
in the present — are among those things preserved in the pyramid of
unknown origin, as yet, but in the storehouse of records.   275-33

In this the entity gained, and in the application of healing did the
entity excel; and in the pyramids yet to be discovered may much of that
compounded by the entity be made to be worth while, even to those of
the day when this *is* found, for those of the entity's *building* may be still
read.   99-6

Mortal Remains

The sands of Giza are said to cover tombs which contain the
mortal remains of many prominent personages of that great Egyptian
State.

Also the buildings pertaining to the preparation much of the tombs of
the peoples of the day were a portion of the entity's activity.   1011-1

. . . the entity was in the Egyptian land during those periods when the
natives were being trained for vocational activities, when there were those
drawings made for the edifices being prepared for halls, for tombs, for the
varied groups that were active during those transition periods following
the period of Ra Ta — who had changed those activities.   3460-1

Embalming was practiced in this period and bodies were elabo-
rately laid in tombs.

. . . the entity became an aid in those that separated into the various
groups and into the establishing of the hospitalization, in the study of that
which was later discovered by those who were called the father of medicine, the father of the healing arts. For then the entity became the re-
nowned one of the embalmers of Egypt.   1334-1

[The entity was] an assistant to him who gave the first of the appliances to preserve men's bodies.   39-2

The entity was one in authority pertaining to the making of fine
linens and especially pertaining to those that were a part of the bindings
about those who were prepared for burial . . .   1603-1

The entity was among the first to make the golden caskets or the
golden bands about those put into the burial chambers.   1561-1

Q-6. [182] as Aardhai — soothsayer.

A-6. As the assistant in the setting of the diagrams of the rebuilded walls of burial, and an astrologer and soothsayer of the day . . .   341-9

The body of Araaraart lies today in one of the hidden pyramids at Giza.

The entity then in the name as called Araaraart . . . The entity, then, in the upper chamber of the northeast corner of the first pyramid builded, there placed by the grandson, the king who afterward ascended to the throne in Egypt — Azorut.   341-8

Q-1. Did this ruler have any other names or titles?

A-1. There were many titles given in the various dialects of the peoples. This is one as will be found as recorded with that of the other rulers. 341-9

The mortal remains of others from that period were placed with that of Araaraart — in his pyramid-tomb.

. . . and the entity [Artexi] gained through this period; and that physical of the entity through that experience may yet be found in the pyramid of the king of the day, yet not uncovered in this day.   2709-1

. . . and there may still be seen in the tomb of the king of the day those expressions of the entity's self in that period [in the name Exli], the mound [not] yet uncovered, but facing that of the Mystery [the Sphinx].   5540-5

The entity among those that were *buried* in the tomb, or in those that are [not] yet uncovered — yet faces the Sphinx, and is the nearest of those buried in that mount. In the name Ar-Kar.   1717-1

Q-7. Where are those records or tablets made of that Egyptian experience, which I might study?

A-7. In the Tomb of Records, as indicated. For the entity's tomb then was a part of the Hall of Records, which has not yet been uncovered. It lies between — or along that entrance from the Sphinx to the temple — or the pyramid; in a pyramid, of course, of its own.   2329-3

History

Most important in the record chambers are, of course, the tablets and writings which relate not only a history long forgotten, but also the spiritual laws of reincarnation. The records at Giza contain both the history of Atlantis (which even includes an account of the beginnings of humanity, the pre-dawn of that civilization) and the history of the Ra Ta period.

Aassa was the historian who compiled much of the material pertaining to the Egyptian period.

. . . the entity was as the recorder of conditions then in the land now known as Egypt. The entity then the historian, the writer of the day, and many of those writings as made by the entity were destroyed in the Memphis and Alexandrian libraries; yet some may yet be found in those casements in the pyramid [not] yet uncovered. In that period the entity gave most to the peoples through the ability to coordinate the teachings of the land and the teachings of those in power. Even when the division arose, the entity able to record the actions of each division without showing favor or partiality in either division. Hence the entity was accorded a place of power, position, during that period, by the ruler and by the seer and by him who was ruled as of power in the beginning of this rule. In the name Aassa.   31-1

The Egyptian records include the writings and tenets of the native scribe, Aarat.

. . . the entity [Aarat] occupied the position of a Jefferson to the Declaration of Independence to the peoples in the religion and in the civil sense . . . The records of much of the scribe may yet be found — many of the tenets were the lessons that the five nations, that gathered later, studied.   900-275

The records include various writings of historical interest. For instance, those of Ilto, a prisoner who sought to explain his position.

In the misuse of the power gained, when the Priest was again in power, the entity lost through the oppressing of those that would speak ill against self or any associated with self. In the name Ilto, and much of the entity's attempts in explaining of position while imprisoned may still be found in that mound not yet uncovered, erected during that period for the king that ruled the land.   417-1

The Atlantean records were stored in three places in the world. One set was sealed in the lost Temple of Iltar in Yucatan, another in Atlantis itself, now submerged, and the third beneath the Sphinx at Giza.

Q-4. In which pyramid or temple are the records mentioned in the readings given through this channel on Atlantis, in April, 1932 [364 series]?

A-4. As given, that temple was destroyed at the time there was the last destruction in Atlantis.

Yet, as time draws nigh when changes are to come about, there may be the opening of those three places where the records are one, to those that are the initiates in the knowledge of the One God:

The temple by Iltar will then rise again. Also there will be the opening of the temple or hall of records in Egypt, and those records that were put into the heart of the Atlantean land may also be found there — that have been kept, for those that are of that group.

The records are One.   5750-1

Hept-Supht was in charge of the placing of these records:

[The entity] aided much in the records; not only of the period but as to how the varied activities were to be in the land pertaining to the records of that which was to be, as well as that which had been, and the records in that monument or tomb or pyramid yet to be opened. Records also of those that were transferred from the destruction of the Atlantean land.

378-13

The records were composed with a combination of Egyptian and Atlantean writing forms.

The entity was a priestess in the Law of One, and among those who — ill — came into the Egyptian land, as the elders in those groups for preserving the records, as well as for preserving a portion of that race, that peoples.

With the periods of reconstruction after the return of the Priest, the entity joined with those who were active in putting the records in forms that were partially of the old characters of the ancient or early Egyptian, and part in the newer form of the Atlanteans.

These may be found, especially when the house or tomb of records is opened, in a few years from now.   2537-1

In those periods the entity persuaded many of those to make for the activities that would preserve to the peoples what would be in the present termed recipes or placards and drawings, and the like, that were the first of such intents brought to the Egyptian peoples (to be sure, not to the Atlanteans, but to the natives and those who had joined there to preserve such records) and the first attempt to make for a *written* language.   516-2

The readings suggest a remarkable feature of these records — that they contain the information telling how they will be reopened in the future.

Q-2. Give in detail what the sealed room contains.

A-2. A record of Atlantis from the beginnings of those periods when the Spirit took form or began the encasements in that land, and the developments of the peoples throughout their sojourn, with the record of the first destruction and the changes that took place in the land, with the record of the *sojournings* of the peoples to the varied activities in other lands, and a record of the meetings of all the nations or lands for the activities in the destructions that became necessary with the final destruction of Atlantis and the buildings of the pyramid of initiation, with who, what, where, would come the opening of the records that are as copies from the sunken Atlantis; for with the change it must rise (the temple) again.

This in position lies, as the sun rises from the waters, the line of the shadow (or light) falls between the paws of the Sphinx, that was later set as the sentinel or guard, and which may not be entered from the connecting chambers from the Sphinx's paw (right paw) until the *time* has been fulfilled when the changes must be active in this sphere of man's experience.

Between, then, the Sphinx and the river.   378-16

The readings repeatedly stress that these records will not be revealed until the time is right.

As for the physical records — it will be necessary to wait until the full time has come for the breaking up of much that has been in the nature of selfish motives in the world. For, remember, these records were made from the angle of world movements. So must thy activities be in the present of the universal approach, but as applied to the individual. 2329-3

For, as must be known to all, God IS! And the soul that becomes more and more aware of His, God's, use of man, that all may know of His Presence, is becoming then in at-onement; as self was in the experience, and preserved that record for the future entering souls, that will be physically known when time has set its mark. 378-1

This may not be entered without an understanding, for those that were left as guards may *not* be passed until after a period of their regeneration in the Mount, or the fifth root race begins. 5748-6

CONSUMMATION

... there were the joining together of forces and all gathered about that plat builded in the holy city between the facing of what afterward became the Sphinx and the holy mount as builded in the manner in which those that were blessed in the period were reposed. 457-2

When the Great Pyramid was completed, a glorious and profound ceremony took place in the Holy City of Aicerao. The capstone was put in place by Hept-Supht, a man who symbolized the passing of the old Atlantean Age and the beginning of a new era.

Much might be given respecting the activities of the entity who sealed with the seal of the Alta and Atlanteans, and the aid given in the completion of the pyramid of initiation as well as in the records that are to be uncovered ...

In describing, then, the ceremonies of dedication or of the activities that began with the keeping of the lines of the priests and the initiates in the order according to their adherence to the Law of One that was initiated in the activities of Hept-Supht in this period, the sounding of the head or the top was given to one that acted in the capacity of the headsman — as would be termed in some of those activities of such nature in other portions of the country, or as nations rose in their service of such natures. And the Priest, with those gathered in and about the passage that led from the varied ascents through the Pyramid, then offered there incense to the gods that dwelt among those in their activities in the period of developments of the peoples. 378-16

The apex (that has been long since removed by the sons of Heth [?] [Gen. 10:15]), the crown or apex, was of metal; that was to be indestructible, being of copper, brass and gold with other alloys that were prepared by those of the period.

And, as this was to be (Gizeh we are speaking of) the place for the initiates and their gaining by personal application, and by the journey or journeys *through* the various activities — as in the ceremonial actions of those that became initiates, it became very fitting (to those as in Ra, and those of Ra-Ta Ra) that there should be the crowning or placing of this symbol of the record, and of the initiates' place of activity, by one who represented both the old and the new; one representing then the Sons of the Law in Atlantis, Lemuria, Oz and Og. So, he that keeps the record, that keeps shut, or Hept-Supht, was made or chosen as the one to *seal* that in the tomb.

The ceremony was long; the clanging of the apex by the gavel that was used in the sounding of the placing. Hence there has arisen from this ceremony many of those things that may be seen in the present; as the call to prayer, the church bell in the present, may be termed a descendant; the sounding of the trumpet as the call to arms, or that as revelry; the sound as of those that make for mourning, in the putting away of the body; the sounding as of ringing in the new year, the sounding as of the coming of the bridegroom; *all* have their inception from the sound that was made that kept the earth's record of the earth's building, as to that from the change. The old record in Gizeh is from that as recorded from the journey to Pyrenees; and to 1998 from the death of the Son of Man (as a man).

378-14

Special ceremonies were conducted at the sealing of the record chambers.

In the record chambers there were more ceremonies than in calling the peoples at the finishing of that called the Pyramid. For, here those that were trained in the Temple of Sacrifice as well as in the Temple Beautiful were about the sealing of the record chambers . . .

Then, the *sealings* were the activities of Hept-Supht with Ra Ta and Isi-so [Isis and Iso?] and the king Araaraart, when there were the gatherings of all the peoples for this record sealing; with incense from the altars of the Temple and altars of the cleansings that were opened for their activities in the grounds about this tomb or temple of records; and many were the cleansings of the peoples from those things or conditions that separated them from the associations of the lower kingdoms that had brought those activities in all lands of the worship of Baalilal [Belial? Deut. 13:13] and of the desires as from carnal associations and influences.

The entity Hept-Supht *led* in the keeping of the records and the buildings that were put in their respective actions or places of activity at this time.

This was in the period, as given, of 10,500 years before the entering of the Prince of Peace in the land to study to become an initiate in or through those same activities that were set by Hept-Supht in this dedicating ceremony.

378-16

When the Great Pyramid was completed, Ra's sojourn in Egypt came to an end, for his work had been consummated.

Also there were then with those of Ra born other children, that were to rise in their various capacities, that their activities would be carried on. With this again brought contentions among the civil and political factions of the land. This again brought the disturbing forces in Ra, and there came then that period when all the Pyramid or memorial was complete, that he, Ra, ascended into the mount and was borne away.   294-152

The events of those times became hidden beneath the silent sands which covered the Temples of Beauty and Sacrifice. Yet the vigilant Sphinx and the stately Great Pyramid are left to stand as mysteries until man again discovers his Egyptian Heritage.

Is it not fitting, then, that these must return? as this Priest may develop himself to be in that position, to be in the capacity of a *liberator* of the world in its relationships to individuals in those periods to come; for he must enter again at that period, or in 1998.   294-151

Part Two

EGYPTOLOGICAL CORRELATIONS

INTRODUCTION

Academic Egyptology contends that civilization in the Nile Valley was beginning only around 4,000 B.C. Before this time, according to the traditional view, the existing cultures were of "primitive" form. The data uncovered thus far suggest the Paleolithic, Mesolithic, and Neolithic stages of cultural development. These are characterized by crude hand tools and weapons, pottery painted in "primitive" design, roughly fashioned graves, fertility figures, etc. From the accumulated data, it is maintained that civilization in Egypt began in the South and spread northward until the unification of Upper and Lower Egypt under Menes in the First Dynasty, when the South conquered the North, around 3,400 B.C.

According to recognized Egyptologists, pyramid structure reached a pinnacle around 2,700 B.C., and they assign the Great Pyramid to this period. According to their view, iron was not used in Egypt until 1,500 B.C. Before that it is believed that metallurgy was limited to forming tools from bronze and copper. Electricity is, of course, thought to have been unknown until Ben Franklin flew his kite. The evidence now accepted suggests that before 4,000 B.C. religion consisted of a form of fertility worship.

Therefore, in seeking corroboration of the Ra Ta story from the available archaeological and mythological data we should look for evidence suggesting the following:

1. Advanced technical and artistic development at a predynastic or early dynastic period.
2. Parallels in religious beliefs, ceremony, symbols, literature, and art work.
3. An invasion from the Caucasus and migrations from the West, evidencing Atlantean racial, societal, and physical characteristics.

105

4. Names of gods and early rulers which suggest the principal personages of the Ra Ta story.
5. Mythological renditions of the principal events of the Ra Ta period.
6. Remains of technical and architectural achievements of the Ra Ta period.
7. An explanation for the discrepancies between Academic Egyptological data and that offered in the readings.

The methodology is to review the accumulated data of Academic Egyptology seeking corroboration of the historical saga presented to us through the psychic channel of Edgar Cayce. This is, of course, a methodology different from the usual scientific procedure of building theory from data.

The overriding thesis is that the later dynastic cultures were echoing, in their cultural forms, those events from which they received their impetus — the events of the Ra Ta period.

Chapter One

REFLECTIONS OF THE RA TA PERIOD
IN PROTODYNASTIC REMAINS

If we accept the Ra Ta story as a record of historical fact, one of the most interesting questions which arises is: what happened between the end of that period described in the Cayce readings and the beginning of dynastic Egyptian history as depicted by archaeology?

Those finds which Egyptologists now classify as predynastic or protodynastic consist of stone implements, pottery, graves, and remains of settlements which could be called "primitive." These finds have been grouped together in various cultural complexes which have been named after the places in Egypt where they were found. The complexes include the Tasian, Badarian, Amratian or Nakadan, and Gerzean cultures. All are considered as belonging to the predynastic period which moves from the Neolithic into the Chalcolithic Age. It is thought that they represent the progression of civilization up to the First Dynasty of Mènes, around 3,400 to 3,200 B.C. The earliest date given to these predynastic cultures is 5,000 B.C., and most are assigned an historical position closer to 4,000 B.C. Beyond 5,000 B.C. the archaeological finds (as they have thus far been interpreted) suggest stone age conditions for the inhabitants of the Nile Valley.

Yet the readings describe in elaborate detail an advanced civilization in Egypt at a time 5,000 years earlier than these "predynastic" cultures uncovered by modern archaeologists. What became of the great culture which produced the Temple Beautiful and sent missionaries all over the world? How was it lost (or preserved) during the 5,000 years of historical vacuity which separate the psychic account from the scientific account of Egypt's beginnings?

Certainly we still have the Sphinx and Great Pyramid which the readings claim for the Ra Ta period. However, Egyptologists have good reasons for assigning these monuments to the Fourth Dynasty of 2,700 B.C. For those who take it seriously, the Ra Ta story raises many mysteries which must be solved in order to establish its veracity.

The Palettes

We can begin by examining certain of the archaeological finds of the protodynastic period to determine whether they show possibilities of reflecting the Ra Ta period.

Of particular interest in this regard are the slate palettes which are dated to the protodynastic period, and which have caused considerable controversy among Egyptologists as to their origins and significance. These slate palettes are flat stone implements which were used for grinding certain materials, particularly malachite. The earliest examples are quite plain but in the latter protodynastic and early dynastic periods they become more elaborate with carved relief scenes and discs in the center for the actual grinding. The scenes carved in relief are very important, for, as many of them depict hunting and battle, they seem to be records of historical events. The suggestion here will be that the scenes on these palettes provide a correlation with the Ra Ta story, particularly the methods of warfare employed by Arart's tribe when it conquered Egypt, and the native conditions at that time. The correlation may not be direct; that is, the scenes on the palettes may not be a direct reference to Arart's invasion. What the scenes might suggest, however, are conditions of society and warfare which received their impetus from those conditions described by the readings.

Whatever the connection between the events of the Ra Ta period and the scenes on these palettes may be, the similarities certainly merit consideration. Therefore we should review the following extract from the readings concerning Arart's invasion:

> The people coming in, or the hills people, using the ways of warfare in that of the sling, and of those projections as were fastened to beasts and turning beasts loose on the people, who were *trained* animals to destroy the foes or the enemies of the invaders – and, as is later seen, there becomes much of this same training in the Egyptian hill country, in which animals – bulls, bear, and the leopard, and the hawk, are trained to give the warfare against peoples that would give war to these groups.
>
> The modes of transportation were the end of the lighter-than-air crafts, the floating of wood or timbers in rafts and forms of boats, and beasts of burden, and of afoot – being the war channels, see? and modes of transportation. Little of carriages, or wagons, or slides, had then been introduced by the invaders.

This reading continues, describing the native Egyptian standards:

These were then, when conquered, not a warlike people — one not prepared for defense or of a way of defending self. Weapons only used in agriculture and in building, and these presenting the only modes of defense by the peoples during that period. Those of transportation being by that of the wheel and of the ox, and the beasts that were trained as domestic for the service of agriculture and of building, see?   900-277

In light of this reading, the battle scenes on the palettes become very interesting. A fragment of the bottom portion of one of the palettes depicts forts as squares with a walled enclosure. Inside each square or fort there is an archaic hieroglyph which probably stands for a particular clan or tribe. An animal appears on top of each enclosure, in the act of picking the walls apart with an implement or weapon which looks like a hoe. Different animals are shown in this act of destruction, among them a lion, a hawk or falcon, and a scorpion. Where animals should appear above two of the forts, the piece is missing.

. . . there began then the segregations more into places, homes, and where there had only been forts or temples in the various sections . . .

294-151

The reverse of this fragment shows oxen, cattle, asses, and sheep in horizontal registers. This may represent the booty taken by the conquerers of the fort-people.

Another of these palettes has been called the Two Gazelles Palette because one side shows two gazelles engaged in battle. The opposite side also depicts a battle scene, in which the enemy is being devoured by a lion which is thought to represent the king. Below the lion, birds of prey pursue and attack the enemy.

On yet another fragment of a slate palette, the enemy is shown as being gored by a bull. This bull has also been thought to represent the king; in later times the bull did become a symbol for the pharaoh.

A complete slate palette was recovered and ascribed to a King Narmer of the First Dynasty. (Many believe Narmer to be identical with Menes, the founder of the First Dynasty.) The Narmer palette shows the king wearing the Red Crown of Lower Egypt (North) on one side, and the White Crown of Upper Egypt (South) on the other.

The first side is divided into three registers. In the first register the King with the Red Crown is being led by a group of priests. It is the central and bottom registers which are particularly interesting. The middle of the palette is dominated by two huge beasts with bodies similar to a dog or a lion. The necks of the beasts are long and snake-like, and intertwined in a sort of "8" pattern. The beasts are held with leashes by two attendants who appear quite dwarfed by the size of the beasts.

The bottom register of this side shows a large bull demolishing a town or fort and trampling a victim underfoot.

Some of these symbols, particularly the bull and the intertwined serpentine necks of the beasts, are quite interesting when compared with the following reading extract:

> The entity joined rather with those that had come from the Atlantean land, making of self then a priestess . . . and there still may be seen in some of the mountain fastnesses of that land; particularly in the Upper Nile where there were those activities in the mountains; the images of the entity that are often worshipped — the entrance to the tombs there.
>
> Then the name was Ai-Ellaiin, and the hieroglyphics will be found to be marked as these: The ibex (the bird of same), the hornheaded man, the ibex turned in the opposite direction, *the sacred bull of Ipis* [?], the hooded man as of Ethiopian people, the cross, the serpent (upright), the staff with the symbol (that should be the symbol of the entity throughout its experience) *as the B's turned towards each other — or one upright with two loops on either side of same, with the serpent head two ways from the top of same* [emphasis mine].   559-7

The reverse side of the Narmer Palette shows the King with the White Crown smiting an enemy. To his rear appears his sandal bearer. Archaic hieroglyphs, which are difficult to read (they seem to be a transitional form from rebus writing), appear in front of the king. Among them is a large falcon or hawk, which in the First Dynasty had already become a symbol of royalty. The bottom register shows two corpses of the fallen enemy of the king.

Another palette which shows these beasts with the long serpentine necks is the Oxford Palette which is thought to pre-date the Narmer Palette. Particularly interesting in this piece is the scene at the bottom of the palette. Here hounds attack fleeing ibexes (goats with large curved horns). It should be remembered that, in the Ra Ta story, the ibex was the name and symbol of the principality ruled by Araaraart's brother, Ralij, and that this principality rebelled against the king and was defeated.

This ibex motif also appears on an ivory knife handle from Gebel el-Arak, a predynastic archaeological site in Egypt. This knife is one of the more celebrated predynastic or protodynastic finds. The carved relief on the top of one side shows a male figure subduing two lions. Below this "hero" figure stand two hunting dogs and beneath these are ibexes, one of which is being attacked by a lion.

We should remember that rulers and principalities were often depicted by their animal totems. Therefore this scene could possibly be recalling the dissension between the Ibex kingdom and the central rule of Egypt. The readings indicate that this division flared up time and time again, even after Ra Ta had departed from Egypt.

110

The obverse side of this knife handle shows a water battle in progress. Two different types of boats are shown, one of which is similar to those used in ancient Mesopotamia, particularly on the Tigris River. The other type of boat has the normal appearance of those of the Gerzean predynastic period.

The modes of transportation were the end of the lighter-than-air crafts, the floating of wood or timbers in rafts and forms of boats . . .   900-277

Of all these protodynastic palettes, one called the Lion or Hunter's Palette is the most interesting, due to its unique characteristics. As its name implies, the relief carved on this palette depicts a hunting scene. The shape of this piece is an elongated triangle. As opposed to the other palettes, one side is left completely blank. It is the only palette in which the scenes are arranged vertically along the longer edges; all the others have the scenes arranged across the face, sometimes in horizontal registers. There is no figure in the scenes which is given particular importance by showing it larger than the other figures, as is the case in the other palettes.

Along each edge of the Hunter's Palette there appears a line of men who carry an assortment of weapons including a lasso. They are dressed in costumes that are unlike any others depicted in archaic times. These consist of short folded skirts fastened by a wide belt with the tail of an animal attached to the back of the belt. These hunters are portrayed with long hair or wigs into which feathers are stuck.

Animals are shown between the two files of hunters. Dogs chase antelopes, a stag, an ostrich, and a hare. The animals appear to tumble over each other and the lions in the scene are maimed, having been shot with many arrows.

The fact that these lions are shown as maimed by the hunters makes this palette unique. Because the lion symbolized the king none of the other archaic, Old, or Middle Kingdom hunting scenes shows the lion being threatened by hunters. Usually the lion remains completely untouched by those around him. That the Hunter's Palette depicts the lions as being severely attacked is even more interesting in view of the fact that it was uncovered with the Two Gazelles Palette wherein the lion completely dominates the scene of the slaughter.

Small hieroglyphs are shown at the larger far end of the Hunter's Palette. These consist of a bull with two heads, or two bulls shown from the front. Beside this sign there appears a small house or temple. It is thought that these hieroglyphs may signify the god to whom the palette is dedicated, along with his temple. Again the palette is unique in the fact that these signs are very small and inconspicuous, whereas in other palettes the figures of the gods appear quite large, dominating the top of the palette. It has also been suggested that these signs signify the place, or nome (province) in Egypt where the hunt took place. If this is so, the signs seem to match those which stood for the Third Nome in the Delta during archaic times.

In attempting to correlate the Hunter's Palette with the Ra Ta story we must speculate a bit. First we would direct our attention to the fact that the hieroglyphs point to the Delta in the North as the place where the events shown in the reliefs took place. This is, of course, the region ruled by Araaraart, who centered his rule near Giza. Then we must remember that this King had to deal with rebellions against his throne — both the Ibex rebellion and the Oelom revolution.

Perhaps the scenes on this palette are a distant record of some of the events of Araaraart's rule, prepared thousands of years later when those events were already mythologized by the creators of the palettes whom Egyptologists know as the predynastic inhabitants of Egypt. The fact that the lion, which would represent the king, is wounded may signify a totemistic portrayal of the rebellions raised against Araaraart. The Two Gazelles Palette which accompanied the Hunter's Palette in the archaeological findings shows the king, as a lion, dominating the battle scene. Perhaps there was originally a series of palettes commemorating the events of Araaraart's rule. The Two Gazelles Palette might, then, signify Araaraart's victory over the rebellious forces.

The opinions of established Egyptologists concerning the origins and significance of the Hunter's Palette are important for this endeavor. In *The Cultures of Prehistoric Egypt*, Elise Baumgartel reports that various scholars attribute the work to Lybians or Syrians, noting that it is probably the oldest known palette in existence. Baumgartel continues, pointing out that the palette is almost certainly Lower Egyptian, from a culture predating the Menes and vastly superior to its Upper Egyptian contemporaries: "The style of relief, with its deep undercutting of the stone and its summary and rather untidy rendering of the figures, shows a knowledge of the technique of relief-working far beyond that available to any archaic artist."[1]

From the readings:

> . . . the entity was in that now known as the Egyptian land, among those peoples that journeyed to Egypt from that known as the Atlantean land . . . Hence the entity was in that position, from that expected and also the developments materially, to aid the more in counseling with those who carved precious stones, those who set about work with the semi-precious stones and regular building stones . . .   984-1

Chapter Two

MYTHOLOGICAL VESTIGES OF RA TA

The readings say that after Ra Ta's banishment and physical regeneration he became known as Ra. In Egyptian mythology this
name is not hard to find; indeed the god Ra occupies a place of great
prominence in the dynastic pantheons as the chief royal deity and
supreme god of the Sun (or light).

The attempt here is to find attributes of Ra which may echo the
name and personality of Ra Ta as given by the readings.

Rosta

The names Re-stew, Ra-sheta, Re-stau, or Rosta, appear quite often
in the dynastic religious literature (*The Book of the Dead* and the
Pyramid Texts). All of these are variations on the same name. During
the dynasties, Rosta referred to a sanctuary in Am Tuat, or the
Underworld, which was intimately connected with the deepest mysteries of Egypt. As the Underworld was, for the Egyptians, a sort of
duplication of the land of Egypt, there was also a "real" or physical
sanctuary of Rosta somewhere in the country.

In the texts Rosta was also closely associated with Sokaris, the
god of the mysteries and geodetic orientation. There are a number of
instances where the dead declare that they have learned the mysteries
of the Underworld and beheld the mysteries of Ra-sheta (Re-stew),
i.e.,the domain of Sokaris, and seen the faces of the gods. The sanctuary associated with this activity is Re-stew, believed to be near
Giza or Saqqara.[2]

Phonetically at least, the name Rosta, or Re-stau, is similar to
Ra Ta. In addition it is interesting that the sanctuary of Rosta is

thought to be near Saqqara, which is a short distance south of Giza, or at Giza itself, which was (according to the readings) the religious center of the Ra Ta period. Also of significance is the fact that the name Rosta was associated with the Mysteries, particularly with Sokaris, the god of the Mysteries.

Sokaris was also a god of geodetic orientation, as Livio Catullo Stecchini, Professor of Ancient History at William Paterson College and an expert on ancient measures, has pointed out. He further relates that both Giza and Saqqara are geodetic centers, and that such places were considered sacred by the dynastic Egyptians. As shown elsewhere (see pp. 128-29) the Inventory Stela found at Giza, which purports to be the work of Khufu (4th Dynasty), makes reference to an "Osiris of Rosta."

In summation, in the name Rosta there is a mixture of conceptions dealing with geodetic focal points, particularly the area around Giza, the Mysteries, and perhaps a connection with the Sphinx.

The Legend of Ra and Isis

This popular legend of the dynastic Egyptians possibly reflects some of the events of the Ra Ta story. The legend of Ra and Isis became popular in Egypt many thousands of years later than the time of Ra Ta, and therefore, as a *legendary* account of Ra and Isis, the events would be, of course, greatly distorted from that which actually took place as given in the readings.

Synopsis: Isis is seen as a sorceress who concerns herself with matters of the spirits and gods. To increase her power, she conspires to learn the secret name of Ra, who has become old and feeble. Towards this end Isis poisons Ra with a serpent. Ra is then in extreme anguish, and none of his fellow gods can help him. Finally, Isis, after making Ra reveal his hidden and august name, cures him with her words of power.

A possible interpretation of this legend in light of the readings can be made: It reflects the conspiracy against Ra Ta, wherein Isis was the bait. Ra is pictured as old and feeble, as was Ra Ta during his banishment in Nubia, when it was felt that he would not be able to carry on the work at hand. The snake, as in the case of Adam and Eve, represents the sexual or carnal nature of the conspiracy and transgression. In the eventual healing of Ra, the archetypes which function in the myth are much like those in the Ra Ta story; in both cases Isis can be seen as the personification of the anima (the woman within man as formulated by Jung) and Ra as the personification of

114

the animus (the man within woman). The myth seems to reflect the scheming, almost destructive side of the anima but, as in the Ra Ta story, a healing wholeness is achieved when the anima and animus are brought into balance in a legitimate fashion. The legend of Ra and Isis, then, presents an archetypal parallel to the story of Ra and Isis as given in the readings.

The Book of the Dead

The first laws, then, partook of that of the study of self, the division of mind, the division of the solar systems, the division of man in the various spheres of existence through the earth plane and through the earth's solar system. *The Book of the Dead,* then, being the first of those that were written as the inscribed conditions necessary for the development in earth or in spirit planes.   5748-2

This reading concerns the original formulation of *The Book of the Dead,* undertaken at a great convention in the Nile Valley in a primeval period. Other readings state that *The Book of the Dead* received additions during the Ra Ta period, many millenia later, in 10,500 B.C. It is known by Egyptologists that *The Book of the Dead* received additions and possibly alterations at various times throughout the dynastic period. Nevertheless, the excerpt above serves as an apt description of this ancient religious text as it appears today.

It is difficult to date *The Book of the Dead,* because of fragmentary evidence and numerous changes known to have been made, but Budge and other scholars agree that at least parts of the text date back to the predynastic period.

Divisions of the Self

The readings state that the first laws which made up the original *Book of the Dead* were concerned with "the division of mind, the division of the solar systems, the division of man in the various spheres of existence through the earth plane and through the earth's solar system." (5748-2) Contemporary knowledge of *The Book of the Dead* indicates that the dynastic Egyptians believed in the following divisions of the Self:

a. *Khat* — the physical body of man considered as a whole.

b. *Ab* — the heart, the source of life, good and evil, and the conscience. It was the heart that was weighed before Osiris to determine if the individual was "justified," and worthy of entrance to Heaven.

c. *Ka* — translated "double," this was an ethereal alter-ego which could leave the body in the tomb and inhabit any statue of the deceased. This life-form could also enjoy life with the gods in Heaven.

d. *Ba* — the heart-soul, which could assume material and non-material forms. It enjoyed eternal existence, and could unite with or leave the body at will. It was for the Ka and Ba that food offerings were left in the tomb, so they would not have to scavenge among the living for food.

e. *Khaibit* — associated with the Ba, "the shadow" could also leave the body at will and travel wherever it pleased.

f. *Sekhem* — "vital force" or "life-force" of the individual. It is believed to dwell in Heaven with the Khu. It is a term translators are hard put to define.

g. *Khu* — the spirit-soul, the immortal part of man which went to Heaven as soon as the body died.

h. *Sahu* — the lasting, incorruptible spirit-body, which incorporated all the ethereal elements of man within it.

i. *Ren* — the name of a man, believed to dwell in Heaven. The Egyptians were very careful to preserve their names because they believed that one existed only as long as his name was preserved.

According to Budge, "the whole man consisted of a natural body, a Spirit-body, a heart, a double, a Heart-soul, a shadow, a Spirit-soul, and a name. All these were, however, bound together inseparably, and the welfare of any single one of them concerned the welfare of all."[3]

The Journey Through Am Tuat

. . . and the entity would do well to study even *The Book of the Dead,* as it was called in the present — yet in that experience it was rather the Book of Life; or it represents that which is the experience of a soul in its sojourn not only in the land of Nirvana [?], the land of Nod, or the land of night, but rather those things that make for the cleansing of a physical body for the aptitudes of expression through the senses or the emotions in the physical forces to the spiritual truths. 706-1

During the dynastic periods (4,000 B.C. until 525 B.C.), Egyptian mythology, as seen in *The Book of the Dead,* divided the land of Am Tuat (i.e., the Underworld), or the Kingdom of Osiris, into regions or sections, sometimes seven in number. Each of these represented a gate, or way which had to be passed by utilizing certain knowledge which pertained to each gate. Passing all of the gates was necessary if one hoped to reach the "City of God."

Each region was called an "Arit," or "Mansion," each having a gatekeeper and a herald. The gatekeeper kept watch and announced the arrival of the traveler, and the herald asked the name of the traveler and interviewed him, reporting all this to his companions. To gain admission to the seven Arits, the soul had to state the names of the gatekeeper and herald of each, and recite a ritual formula to convince them of its good faith.[4]

This concept of the seven gates or Arits, which was popular thousands of years after the Ra Ta period, provides an interesting comparison with the following extract from the readings concerning the Temple Beautiful:

> From station to station in the seven phases or seals or stands or places of the activities, they were such as to make each station lead from one to another by ever crossing the one; making the continued web.

> *Q-3. [585]: What part did I take in services in the Temple Beautiful?*
> A-3. The Announcer with the cymbal and horn.

> *Q-4. [5773]: Please give me the information as to whether or not I was in the Temple Beautiful. If so, please give that service which I rendered.*
> A-4. An observer of those seals wherein the effects of the sojourns in the varied activities were to be seen, or the effects from the planetary sojourn. Hence a *keeper* of seals there.   281-25

The Fifth Hour of Am Tuat

As noted, the Egyptian concept of the Underworld, Am Tuat, had this realm divided into regions called Arits. Sometimes the Underworld was depicted in temporal rather than spatial terms; then the gates or Arits became the hours of Am Tuat. Each hour contained specific deities and sacred activities pertinent to the soul's journey. Each soul, in its journey through Am Tuat, was identifying with the god Ra, who, as the sun-god, entered the realm of night (Underworld) after each day, at sunset.

The dynastic Egyptians often painted scenes or vignettes which depict the different phases of the Am Tuat journey described in *The Book of the Dead.*

The Fourth and Fifth Hours of Am Tuat, as described and depicted in *The Book of the Dead,* exhibit features which may be important as mythological correlates of the Ra Ta story. In the Fourth and Fifth Hours the deceased (Ra) is entering the domain of Sokaris, who is the god of Egypt's deepest mysteries. These Hours are closely connected with the name Rosta. In light of the readings' story of Egypt and the founding of the Sphinx and the Pyramid, interesting correlations may be drawn.

C.J. Bleeker, Professor of the History of Religions at the University of Amsterdam, discusses the Fourth and Fifth Hours of Am Tuat in his analysis of the Sokaris festival. In his book, *Egyptian Festivals,*

Enactments of Religious Renewal, he explains that Sokaris and his realm symbolize an aspect of the Underworld which, as pictured and described, is inscrutable even to Ra. The vignette shows Sokaris as sealed off and physically inaccessible; in fact, the inscriptions tell the reader that Ra may only speak to Sokaris. They read: "The secret roads of Re-stew. The double gates of the god. He, the sun-god, does not pass through them; his voice it is that they [Sokaris and his companions] hear."

The symbolism used in Sokaris' realm should be noted. At top center, the scarab (symbol of the sun) emerges from under a bell-shaped object designated by the hieroglyphs for the dark of night; i.e., in the darkness of night, the sun rises. Under this symbol is the abode of Sokaris, whose physical presence within the ellipse is shown by the sand he stands on (dots), and the inscription which places his "flesh" within the ellipse. The exact significance of the two-headed snake he stands on is unclear, but the snake is described as "the many-coloured feathered one . . . He lives from the breath of his mouth, every day. What he must do is to protect his [Sokaris'] image." Another of Sokaris' guardians is Aker, the earth-god whose two lion-headed figures rest, Sphinx-like, at either end of the ellipse. The inscriptions say that the realm is shrouded in complete darkness, except for the light which emanates from Sokaris himself. Above the ellipse is a hill surmounted by a female head. This symbol is identified as "the body of Isis, who is above the sand of Sokaris." When correlated with less distinct symbols, this symbol evokes a mythical aspect of Isis, in which she is fecundated by the dead Osiris, thus generating life in death.

The symbolism here expresses the inscrutable aspect of Sokaris: he is the one who possesses the ability to give life, and can generate life in death. By combining and juxtaposing symbols from two separate myths, the Egyptians have expressed their concept of Sokaris more clearly and subtly than they could have with words.[5]

Professor Stecchini views the Fifth Hour of Am Tuat and the god Sokaris from a different perspective. He sees Sokaris as a god of orientation and the Fifth Hour in its geodetic aspects. He points out that Sokar, as he was known in the Old Kingdom, was the god of orientation and cemeteries. The god's symbol was the same as that used for a geodetic marker, resembling the bell-shaped object above the mound of Isis in the illustration. The two birds perched on this *omphalos* [Grk. "navel"] are usually found in this symbol of Sokaris. In standard iconography, they stand for the delineation of the earth's meridians and parallels.[6]

It is tempting to see in this symbolically pregnant Fifth Hour of

Am Tuat many reflections of the Ra Ta period and the significance which this saga places on the ancient Giza monuments. The suggestion is that the mysteries which are cryptically conveyed in the Fifth Hour refer to the mysteries of the Sphinx, the Great Pyramid, and the Hall of Records. This comes to light if, keeping the readings' story in mind, we view Sokaris as the deification of those mysteries.

Bleeker observes that Sokaris' realm is "hermetically sealed"; this could be a reference to the Hall of Records which was "hermetically" sealed by Hept-Supht. This possibility is indicated in the hieroglyphic text by, "the upper half of the secret cavern of Sokaris who is on his sand." It is interesting that in the vignette Sokaris is shown as standing on sand (depicted by dots), while at the same time he is shown as being covered by sand.

Stecchini has pointed out how the "bell-shaped object" actually functions as an *omphalos,* a marker for geodetic focal points. (These objects were also found at Thebes, considered a geodetic focus after the Twelfth Dynasty moved the capital there, and at the ruins of Delphi in Greece, the city known as the "navel of the world.") The presence of the *omphalos* in the Fifth Hour adds weight to the suggestion that the symbology therein is focused on Giza, for the Great Pyramid is situated with exceptional accuracy on the 30th parallel and the prime meridian of Egypt. It is also accurately oriented to true north: its diagonals, if projected, neatly contained the entire region of the Delta. Furthermore, on an equal-surface projection of the earth's land mass, the center appears where the Great Pyramid is located at Giza.

The snake upon which Sokaris stands, who "guards his image," may be a symbolic reference to the "guardians" said by the readings to have been left at the Hall of Records:

> . . . there is a chamber or passage from the right forepaw to this entrance of the record chamber, or record tomb. This may not be entered without an understanding, for those that were left as guards may *not* be passed until after a period of their regeneration in the mount, or the fifth root race begins.   5748-6

It is tempting to see the lion figures of Aker as a representation of the Sphinx at Giza, since other aspects of this Hour point in that direction. If this is the case, we then have the Sphinx guarding the figure of Sokaris, the personification of the mysteries, i.e., the secret chambers of the Record Tomb.

Budge notes that the lion was one of the more prominent figures in Egyptian symbology, even in the Early Empire. Aker was the god who guarded the gates of morning and evening, and for this reason the Egyptians placed figures of him at their palace and tomb doors to ward off evil spirits, both in and out of the flesh. These figures of Aker were often given the heads of men and women, and are commonly known to us by the name given them by the Greeks — "Sphinx."[7]

From the readings comes another interesting correlation with the Fifth Hour, the Sphinx, and Aker:

> The entity among those that were *buried* in the tomb, or in those that are not yet uncovered — yet faces the Sphinx, and is the nearest of those buried in that mount. In the name Ar-Kar . . . 1717-1

Immediately over Sokaris' ellipse is the hill with a female head at the apex. Although the texts refer to the hill as "the body of Isis," we may see here a depiction of the Pyramid. This suggestion has the weight of the *omphalos* above the "hill" in the scene, which, standing for geodetic focal points, would characterize the Pyramid below it as such if this part of the scene points to the Great Pyramid at Giza. That Isis' head should appear above the "Pyramid" is significant in view of what the readings say about her fulfilling an advisory function with the building of the monument, and it might be remembered that the Inventory Stela refers to Isis as the "Mistress of the Pyramid."

Composite Beings

The biological conditions which produced "animal appendages" on the bodies of many individuals in the Ra Ta period could very well be reflected in the composite beings which were rendered in dynastic mythology.

Composite beings have always figured as predominant images in the religion and mythology of ancient Egypt. This is seen in the renderings of the most important deities such as Thoth with the head of an ibis-bird and the body of a man, Anubis with the head of a jackal and the body of a man, Amen-Ra in his hawk-headed form, and many others. These mythological forms consisted of joining an animal form with the human body or connecting two different creatures into one being.

Budge notes that many ancient writers such as Pliny, Diodorus, and Strabo gave long descriptions of these composite beings, particularly the Sphinx, apparently taking for granted that such creatures actually existed. To this he adds that the Egyptians themselves tenaciously retained such composite representations long after they could have believed in their reality, despite the ridicule of foreigners.[8]

Archaeological data suggest that belief in composite beings was prevalent in predynastic times. Bird-headed figures with human bodies were found in predynastic graves from the Nakada I culture.[9]

The Electric Surgical Knife

Egyptian funerals during the dynastic period were very elaborate and involved extensive ritual. The Ceremony of Opening the Mouth, which was performed at the door of the tomb, was one of the rites of purification wherein the deceased's mouth was opened so that he would be able to speak in Am Tuat, or the Other World. This ceremony was performed with a particular instrument, and its description from the religious texts is very interesting in view of the electrical knife developed by Asphar and Ajax-Ol in the Ra Ta period.

From the texts: "May the god Ptah open my mouth, and may the god of my city loose the swathings, even the swathings which are over my mouth . . . May my mouth be opened, may my mouth be unclosed by Shu [or Ptah] with his iron knife wherewith he opened the mouth of the gods."[10]

Immediately following the application of these metallic instruments, the ceremony involves certain acts of purification. We should remember that the electrical knife of the Ra Ta period was used for the purifications which were conducted in the Temple of Sacrifice.

It may also be significant that the metal from which the instrument (in the Ceremony of the Opening of the Mouth) is composed is called the iron which came forth from Set (or Seth). As discussed elsewhere, Set, and his followers termed the Sethites, may be a later mythological form of the Atlanteans. The electric surgical knife was developed from Atlantean technique, and one of its inventors, Ajax-Ol, was an Atlantean.

Budge reports that the Ceremony of the Opening of the Mouth dates from the end of the Neolithic Period in Egypt, making it one of the oldest known Egyptian ceremonies. The texts indicate that this ceremony was performed on the gods when they were created, and was a part of the funeral service for any mortal who could afford the cost.[11]

Chapter Three

PREDYNASTIC SOCIETY

Certain aspects of social life in predynastic Egypt, evidenced by modern archaeological discoveries, show strong parallels to the development of society in the Ra Ta period.

Race

During the Ra Ta period, physical characteristics became extremely varied because of migrations and numerous racial groups which were common throughout most of Egypt's history. During the dynasties, however, fair skin and blond hair were generally unknown. The only unusual exceptions are those found in paintings on the walls of Fourth Dynasty tombs, mainly located at Giza.

We should note that Egyptologists believe these traits signify Libyan origins for those so depicted in the paintings, or that the individuals were wearing wigs.

William Flinders Petrie notes that there seem to be three distinct races depicted in the ancient Egyptian portraiture, especially that of the Fourth Dynasty. The ruling class has features similar to those from the "divine land" of Punt, who probably entered Egypt in the Nile valley at Koptos, coming from the Red Sea. The upper class seems to resemble people from the Tell Lo region in Mesopotamia; other influences in Egypt from this region strengthen the theory that migration probably occurred from there. The lower classes show Negroid features, suggesting that Negro or mulatto races are Egypt's oldest inhabitants. There are also definite signs of Libyan influence. Strangely enough, although fair skin and blond hair were almost unheard of in Egypt, one picture of Hetepheres II, daughter of

Khufu, shows her with distinctly blond hair. Another figure, also named Hetep-heres, perhaps the granddaughter of the first, is also depicted with yellow hair. [12]

Atlantean Vestiges

Q-7. Are the following the correct places? Atlantean the red?
A-7. Atlantean and America, the red race. 364-13

From predynastic time and throughout the dynastic period comes evidence of people with red racial characteristics. Because such people were always an extreme minority, or an exception to the common racial characteristics, and for reasons unknown, these people were considered to possess certain magical or religious significance.

Representations of these red race characteristics have been uncovered from periods of great antiquity. Predynastic figurines of men and women have been found from the Badarian, Nakada I, and Nakada II cultural complexes. These often have the face and body painted red. According to Elise Baumgartel, "the ancient Egyptians were in the habit of painting themselves with red and green make-up since Badarian days . . . " [13] Budge mentions that the wall paintings in Egyptian tombs "often contain representations of men whose bodies are coloured red, and in papyri containing vignettes of *The Book of the Dead* the body of Osiris is frequently given this colour. From these it is clear that the Egyptians were in the habit of painting their bodies with red pigment . . . " [14]

Atlanteans, Caucasians, and the Sky Religion

G.A. Wainwright, in *The Sky Religion in Egypt,* discusses the Sky Religion as opposed to the Solar cults which centered around Heliopolis. He proposes that in the early prehistory of Egypt the inhabited regions of that area were to the west of the Nile valley in what is now called Libya. At that time what is now desert was fertile.

As life in the Sahara became more difficult, those natives (Badarians, Amratians, and Gerzeans) began to move toward the Nile. With them they brought their religion, which centered around the sky and its rain-giving capacities. Once in the Nile region, the sky was no longer regarded strictly as a source of water, and sun worship began to develop. However, both gods, Set (of storms) and Min (of the sun), survived throughout pharaonic history. It is not too difficult to conceive of the fabled battles between Horus (god of the sky) and Set (god of storms, disasters, and ill fate) as symbolic of the clashes between tribes with different religious systems symbolized by the combatant gods. [15,16]

Petrie goes on to assign the different classes of gods to the various races of peoples entering Egypt around this early time. To the Libyans he assigns a class of gods containing Set, Neith, Osiris, Isis, Amen, and Khonsu. He notes that all these gods were depicted as men and women with human passions and actions, having no mystic significance in and of themselves. However, he also notes a large group of gods with considerably more "cosmic" significance, representing elements of nature — earth, air, sky, and sun — whose abode, Heliopolis, was a center of theology and literature. These gods, too, were primarily human in form, although Petrie sees their origin as linked to Mesopotamia. He proposes that Heliopolis was at one time a center of power of the eastern invaders who introduced these deities.[17]

The Libyan tribes were of the red race, or those with white skin and red or fair hair. Therefore their central deity, Set, was characterized with these features.

Wainwright points out numerous examples of these red-colored people rising to power throughout the dynasties; and in each case, it seems there was a magical/religious significance attached to these individuals. Moreover, these people all show connections with the old Sky Religion which in its practice seems to have demanded at times the sacrifice of these "red people" to insure fertility.

In times when the old religion, i.e., the Sky Religion, had succeeded in being the dominant religious influence in dynastic Egypt, such sacrifice was even demanded of the king, though these rulers usually sought a ritualistic escape from their fate. The usual method was to identify the ruler with some deity, requiring that another, a mortal, be offered as a sacrifice.

These people, marked by their redness, were called "Followers of Seth," or Typhonians. They survived as a sect until the Nineteenth Dynasty, and were said to have special life spans allotted to them, and certain forms of death, although the details of that are now lost. However, the predominant mark identifying a "Follower of Seth" was his redness.[18]

In light of the Ra Ta story, these Sethites of the Sky Religion may owe their origin to a period much earlier than that which Egyptologists now know as the predynastic period; and their origin would be farther to the west of Egypt than Libya.

The suggestion is that the Sethites with their red race characteristics may have been ancestors of the Atlanteans who migrated to Egypt around 10,500 B.C. The tensions which sometimes resulted between those people already established in Egypt and the immigrating Atlanteans could possibly be echoed in the mythological battles between Horus (the Egyptians and Arart's tribe) and Set (the Atlanteans).

In light of what the readings indicate about the technical superiority and power of the Atlanteans, it seems reasonable that their dynastic descendants should be regarded as carrying religious and magical significance. That the gods of the predynastic western invaders known to Egyptology should manifest "human passions and actions," as Petrie points out, is further indication that these people may have been Atlantean vestiges.

The data indicate that centered at Heliopolis (which is a short distance from the Giza plateau) were an eastern invading people who might have been vestiges of the tribe of Arart. If so, their origin would not be Mesopotamia but the Caucasus regions, according to the readings. It is significant that the data show the gods of these invaders also to be of human form, but carrying cosmic attributes.

Further evidence which points to a connection between the dynastic followers of Set and the Atlanteans comes from the Jewish historian, Josephus: "Now Adam . . . had indeed many other children, but Seth in particular . . . Now this Seth, when he was brought up, and came to those years in which he could discern what was good, became a virtuous man; and as he was himself of an excellent character, so did he leave children behind him who imitated his virtues . . . They also were the inventors of that peculiar sort of wisdom which is concerned with the heavenly bodies and their order. And that their inventions might not be lost before they were sufficiently known, upon Adam's prediction that the world was to be destroyed one time by force of fire, and at another time by the violence and quantity of water, they made two pillars; the one of brick, the other of stone: they inscribed their discoveries on them both, that in case the pillar of brick should be destroyed by the flood, the pillar of stone might remain, and exhibit those discoveries to mankind; and also inform them that there was another pillar of brick erected by them. Now this remains in the land of Siriad to this day."[19]

Communalism

. . . for no merchants then existed, as there was one common store for all.   294-149

There were also established storehouses, that would be called banks in the present, or places of exchange . . .   294-148

The entity was then among those who set about to be in charge over what we would call the granaries, or the places for the preservation of the grains of the land . . .   1587-1

125

In *The Cultures of Prehistoric Egypt,* Elise Baumgartel notes that starting with the Badarian period, granaries were to be found in old settlement sites. These granaries were usually grouped together, not near individual huts, suggesting that the food stores of the community were held to be common property.[20] This suggests an unusually advanced social system of land and food administration, perhaps carried over from the Ra Ta period.

During the dynastic periods women were regarded as equal to men in the home. Inheritance was governed by a system of matrilineal descent. This was even true of inheritance of the throne.[21]

The crowns of both Upper and Lower Egypt were personified in feminine forms: the crown of the north was called the Lady of Spells, and the crown of the south was called the Lady of Dread. Both seem to have been considered guardian-goddesses having divinity in and of themselves. When the two were united into the Double Crown, it was called the Lady of Power or the Lady of Flame.[22] In the Pyramid Texts, the crown is referred to as "the lady."

Women's Position

> ... and those of Isis (now) in the form of the advisor — for the laying in of those things that would present to those peoples the *advancement* of the portion of man, or woman, to her position in the activities of the human race or human experience, these changed the position or attitude of these particular peoples as to the position that was held by woman in her relations to the developing of the conditions that either were to be national, local, or individual ...   294-151

Archaeological data from the predynastic period show that women of the time held advanced social positions. The Great Mother, also symbolized by the cow, was always one of the foremost Egyptian goddesses. Early slate palettes from Gerzeh suggest that, even then, she was regarded as Queen of Heaven. Furthermore, the graves of women from the predynastic period are some of the largest and most elaborate. Judging from the furnishings, ornaments and pottery, some women became princesses, priestesses, or both, and held positions of power and consequence.[23] Baumgartel further speculates that women may have been rulers during this period; to wit, the evidence first points to the probability that the governing body of the time was monarchial, second to the probability that the graves of the monarchs were among the most important and richly furnished, and third to the fact that a high percentage of the richest graves were those of women. She goes on to note that the position of queen during the dynastic periods was quite important, with a queen occasionally assuming the throne as supreme ruler.[24]

This high social position of women continued throughout the later dynastic periods. During these later times, the position of women in society was clearly centered around the goddess Isis.

> This, then, made for an *endowing* of . . . [Isis] to the position of the first goddess that was so crowned, and there was given then that place that was to be sought by others that would gain counsel and advice even from the Priest, gained access through that of Isis to the Throne itself.
>
> 294-151

E.A. Wallis Budge notes that although Isis is one of the most frequently mentioned goddesses in Egyptian writings, little if anything is known about her origin in predynastic times. Although her symbol, ⌂ , is the throne (or seat), Egyptologists are unable to find a rational way of correlating her symbol to any of the attributes commonly ascribed her. Budge says that all attempts to explain the derivation of her symbol in light of accepted information are "mere guesses."[25] He also suggests that the inventors of the oldest company of gods in Egypt were "people in whose households women held a high position, and among whom they possessed more power than is usually the case among Oriental peoples."[26]

Chapter Four

THE MONUMENTS AT GIZA

THE SPHINX

The Inventory Stela, a large stone piece found at Giza, purports to have been made by Khufu (Fourth Dynasty, 3,400 B.C.). Its hieroglyphic carved relief tells of repairs he made on the Sphinx and a Temple of Isis in the area. This is remarkable by present theories because the Sphinx is thought to be the work of Chephren, who succeeded Khufu as Pharaoh, and because Isis is thought to have become a popular deity only in later dynasties. For these reasons, and because the name list, description of the gods, and the hieroglyphic style correspond to the 26th Dynasty, Egyptologists have thought the stela to be at least partly a forgery from that time. The question is, how much of the stela is concocted, and what portion of the text is an exact copy of the original?

The question of the validity of this stela has raised controversy among Egyptologists. Two of the most interesting features of the debate over the stela involve a thunderstorm and a sycamore tree. Selim Hassan, in *The Sphinx, Its History in the Light of Recent Excavations,* points out that there is indeed damage to the Sphinx which could have been caused by lightning as mentioned in the stela inscription, although there is no evidence to attribute this damage (and its repair) to the Khufu period. A sycamore mentioned in the stela, according to Hassan, has "the stamp of truth," especially when one considers that there is a sycamore "of immense age, still flourishing a little to the south of the Sphinx." [27]

He further notes that in nearly all of the stelae bearing reliefs of the Sphinx, the Sphinx is shown resting on a pedestal surmounted by a cornice; and that a number of the reliefs also depict a door, apparently in the pedestal. He explains that this pedestal actually represents the natural rock on which the Sphinx rests, which is cut down to a level of 2.50 meters below the level of the paws. The doorway of the pedestal, he believes, actually represents a niche in the western wall of the court which surrounds the Sphinx.

However, in light of the readings concerning the Record Chamber, there is an alternative explanation for the manner in which the Sphinx is pictured in the reliefs.

> This in position lies, as the sun rises from the waters, the line of the shadow (or light) falls between the paws of the Sphinx, that was later set as the sentinel or guard, and which may not be entered from the connecting chambers from the Sphinx's paw (right paw) until the *time* has been fulfilled when the changes must be active in this sphere of man's experience.   378-16

Several possible correlations can be made with the text of the Inventory Stela and the Ra Ta story. The mention in the stela of "the House of Isis" presents some possibilities in view of the following reading:

> We see this sphinx was builded as this:
>
> The excavations were made for same in the plains above where the temple of Isis had stood . . .   195-14

The fact that the Inventory Stela refers to Isis as the "Mistress of the Pyramid" is interesting in view of the fact that the readings inform us that Isis was an advisor for its construction.

A mention of the "House of Osiris" could refer to Asriaio, the Grand Councilor, whose likeness was put on the Sphinx, the suggestion being that "Osiris" is a mythological carryover of this person who was so important in the Ra Ta period.

The Cayce readings are not the only source of information which attributes the Sphinx to influences outside Egypt. Budge says, "Judging by the silence of the ancient monuments about the Sphinx this figure . . . cannot have been popular in dynastic times, and if this was so, it is possible that it was due to the fact that the Sphinx was thought to be connected in some way with the foreigners or with a foreign religion which dated from pre-dynastic times." [28]

THE GREAT PYRAMID

Since 813 A.D., when the Arab scholar-explorer Al Mamun first blasted an entrance into the upper passages of the Great Pyramid, various researchers have speculated on, and found evidence for, the idea that this pyramid incorporates, in its geometric relationships, knowledge pertaining to astronomy, astrology, mathematics, geodesy and geophysics.

While the various theories proposed cannot be fully elaborated and correlated with the Ra Ta story here, it should be mentioned that they include the following proposals:

That the Great Pyramid functions as:

1. A theodolite for surveying.
2. An almanac and sun dial.
3. A map projection of the Northern Hemisphere.
4. An astronomical observatory.
5. A geodetic marker for latitude and longitude.

Other proposals suggest that the Pyramid incorporates the distance from the Earth to the Sun, mathematical configurations including the Fibbonaci series, *pi, phi,* 2-5-3, 3-4-5 triangle and the Golden Section; and standards of measure, particularly those incorporated in the sarcophagus of the King's Chamber.

Peter Tompkins has presented many of these proposals in his recent popular book, *Secrets of the Great Pyramid.* Thus far, however, most of the more established Egyptologists do not give credence to such proposals, although there is good evidence for some of the theories. The more serious student should study the arguments and decide for himself.

Construction

Scholars have speculated as to why the walls of the passageways are formed with blocks of stone at various angles to one another. Two of the most eminent Egyptologists, Ludwig Borchardt and William Flinders Petrie, have made careful observations of structural variations in the Pyramid.

Petrie was impressed by the fact that in many places the workmanship of the Pyramid was extremely refined while other parts seemed to be crude and unfinished. He concluded that "the architect who designed and insisted on all the fine work died during its progress, and far less able heads were left to finish it."[29]

Borchardt concluded that the angular variations of the blocks which formed the walls of the ascending passage signified a modification of design after the Pyramid was in certain stages of construction. He "deduced that the Pyramid must have already reached a level corresponding to halfway up the as yet nonexistent Ascending Passage before it was decided to use an Upper Chamber," at which point the lower half of the passage was dug through stone laid level to the ground, after which the stone was laid parallel with the passage's slope.[30]

130

In both cases, the scholars do not attribute the "irregularities" in the Ascending Passage to any preconceived plan.

> All changes that came in the religious thought in the world are shown there, in the variations in which the passage through same is reached, from the base to the top — or to the open tomb *and* the top. These are signified by both the layer and the color in what direction the turn is made.   5748-5

Contended Sequential Development

Academic Egyptology traces the development of the pyramid form from the crude mastabas of the First Dynasty to the culmination of the pyramid-temple complex with the pyramids of Khufu and Chephren of the Fourth Dynasty (2,700 B.C.). Crucial to this chronological organization of the data is the Step Pyramid of Zoser, at Saqqara. This is considered the oldest of the pyramids and it is reasonably held that this complex was built in the Third Dynasty, around 3,000 B.C. If, as according to the readings, the Great Pyramid was built in 10,490 B.C., it would, of course, greatly antedate Zoser's pyramid — which is quite contrary to the traditional view that assigns the Great Pyramid to Khufu (also called Cheops), of some 300 years later than Zoser.[31]

This contended sequential development can look quite convincing; however, a study of the interior chambers of the Great Pyramid reveals some unique features. For example, it is the only pyramid with an ascending passageway, and in no other pyramid are the chambers found at such an interior height as the Queen's Chamber and the King's Chamber.[32]

I.E.S. Edwards further relates that pyramids following those of the Giza period tended back toward the Step Pyramid form (pyramids of Djedefre and Nebka — Sixth Dynasty).

Piazzi Smyth, an Astronomer Royal for Scotland in the 1800s, in 1864 was the first researcher to measure the Great Pyramid thoroughly with modern measuring equipment. Through his research he became convinced that the Pyramid had been built by Divine Ordination.[33]

Smyth points out that no graffiti from classical Greek or Roman times are found in the ascending passage, Queen's Chamber, King's Chamber, or Grand Gallery. Nor are there any graffiti of the dynastic Egyptians in these areas. Such graffiti, however, are found in the descending passage and chamber which was sealed off from the upper areas by an indistinguishable trap door. The suggestion is that the dynastic Egyptians' knowledge of the Pyramid's interior consisted only of the descending passage and chamber, and that this is why later pyramids, which were but copies of the Pyramid of Ra Ta (if we accept the readings' chronology), contained only descending passages and chambers.

The Cartouches of Khufu

Egyptologists assign the Great Pyramid to the Fourth Dynasty ruler Khufu. One reason for this is that Herodotus, the Greek historian, records that Khufu was the builder of the Pyramid. But perhaps the strongest reason is that cartouches were found in the Great Pyramid bearing this ruler's name.

Above the King's Chamber are five "relieving" chambers of the same floor dimensions as the King's Chamber but only three feet in height. The first of the five can be entered by way of a narrow passage from the top of the Grand Gallery. The remaining four were entered in modern times by blasting through solid masonry; they could not have been previously entered since the completion of this section of the pyramid. Cartouches were found in these chambers bearing the names of Khufu and an unknown Khum Khuf.

These cartouches were left in a haphazard fashion in the upper relieving chambers above the King's Chamber. Because these chambers could not have been entered since the completion of this portion of the Pyramid, and unless we entertain the idea that this portion of the Pyramid was restored by the Khufu of the Fourth Dynasty, we have to assume (if we accept the readings' account of the Pyramid) that they were put there in the time of Ra Ta. With the cartouches are other hieroglyphs which seem to give directions for the placement of the stones. It is surmised by Egyptologists that these hieroglyphs were done by the workmen when they built this Pyramid for Khufu around 2,700 B.C.

If we take the Ra Ta period as historical fact, then we must entertain the idea — fantastic as it may seem — that these cartouches were placed in the Pyramid by the followers of Ra Ta as a "red herring" for modern man until the time was right for the real meaning of this Pyramid to be brought to light. This, of course, would require considerable prophetic skill. If it is true, however, that these people had the ability to incorporate prophecy in the Pyramid which was so accurate as to name the "hour, day, year, place, country, nation, town, and individuals" (5748-5) of future world events, then perhaps it was possible for them to make such a forecast — not only that thousands of years later there would be a ruler named Khufu, but that thousands of years from the Fourth Dynasty investigators would enter the sealed chambers and find Khufu's name on the wall.

REFERENCES

Part Two — Egyptological Correlations

Chapter One

1. Elise J. Baumgartel, *The Cultures of Prehistoric Egypt,* Vol. II, pp. 61-76.

Chapter Two

2. C.J. Bleeker, *Egyptian Festivals, Enactments of Religious Renewal,* pp. 47, 53.
3. E.A. Wallis Budge, *The Book of the Dead* (1960 ed.), p. 81.
4. Ibid., pp. 268-69.
5. Bleeker, *Egyptian Festivals,* pp. 64-69.
6. Livio Catullo Stecchini, "Notes on the Relation of Ancient Measures to the Great Pyramid," in *Secrets of the Great Pyramid,* p. 298.
7. Budge, *The Gods of the Egyptians,* Vol. II, p. 361.
8. Ibid., Vol. I, pp. 62-63.
9. Baumgartel, *Cultures,* pp. 69-70.
10. Budge, *The Book of the Dead* (1901 ed.), Vol. I, p. 133.
11. Budge, *Dead* (1960), p. 246.

Chapter Three

12. Sir (Wm.) Flinders Petrie, *Religion and Conscience in Ancient Egypt,* pp. 26-27.
13. Baumgartel, *Cultures,* pp. 66, 67.
14. Budge, *Osiris: The Egyptian Religion of Resurrection,* Vol. II, p. 257.
15. Gerald A. Wainwright, *The Sky Religion in Egypt: Its Antiquity and Effects,* pp. 8-11.
16. Petrie, *Religion,* p. 57.
17. Ibid., pp. 57, 78-81.
18. Wainwright, *Sky Religion,* p. 31.
19. Josephus, Book I *(The Works of Flavius Josephus),* p. 43.
20. Baumgartel, *Cultures,* pp. 141, 142.
21. Margaret A. Murray, *The Splendor That Was Egypt,* pp. 100-101.
22. Ibid., p. 179.
23. Baumgartel, *Cultures,* pp. 61, 149.
24. Ibid., pp. 61-76, 142.
25. Budge, *Gods,* Vol. II, p. 202.
26. Ibid., Vol. I, p. 287.

Chapter Four

27. Selim Hassan, *The Sphinx, Its History in the Light of Recent Excavations,* pp. 224-27.
28. Budge, *Gods,* Vol. I, p. 472.
29. Petrie, *A History of Egypt,* Vol. I, p. 59.
30. Peter Tompkins, *Secrets of the Great Pyramid,* p. 239.
31. I.E.S. Edwards, *The Pyramids of Egypt,* p. 116.
32. Ibid., pp. 121-26.
33. Piazzi Smyth, *Our Inheritance in the Great Pyramid,* pp. 219-20.

BIBLIOGRAPHY

Baikie, James. "Sphinx." In James Hastings' *Encyclopedia of Religion and Ethics*. Vol. XI, pp. 767-68. New York: Charles Scribner's Sons, n.d.

Baumgartel, Elise J. *The Cultures of Prehistoric Egypt*. Vol. II. London: Oxford University Press, 1960.

Bleeker, C.J. *Egyptian Festivals, Enactments of Religious Renewal*. Leiden, Netherlands: E.J. Brill, 1967.

Breasted, James Henry. *A History of Egypt*. New York: Charles Scribner's Sons, 1909.

————. *Ancient Records of Egypt*. 5 vols. Chicago: University of Chicago Press, 1906-07.

Budge, E.A. Wallis. *The Book of the Dead*. 3 vols. London: Kegan Paul, Trench, Trübner & Co., Ltd., 1901.

————. *The Book of the Dead*. New Hyde Park, N.Y.: University Books, 1960.

————. *The Gods of the Egyptians*. 2 vols. New York: Dover Publications, Inc., 1969.

————. *Osiris: The Egyptian Religion of Resurrection*. 2 vols. in 1. New Hyde Park, N.Y.: University Books, 1961.

Cerny, Jaroslav. "The Determination of the Exact Size and Orientation of the Great Pyramid of Giza." In *Survey of Egypt*, Paper No. 39. Cairo, 1925.

Edwards, I.E.S. *The Pyramids of Egypt*. Baltimore, Md.: Penguin Books,Inc., 1961.

Emery, Walter B. *Archaic Egypt*. Baltimore, Md.: Penguin Books,Inc., 1961.

————. *Great Tombs of the First Dynasty*. 3 vols. Cairo and London, 1949-58.

Erman, Adolf. *The Ancient Egyptians, A Sourcebook of Their Writings*. New York: Harper Torchbooks, 1966.

Frankfort, Henriette Antonia (Groenewegan). *Arrest and Movement; An Essay on Space and Time in the Representational Art of the Ancient Near East*. New York: Hacker Art Books, 1972.

Gardiner, Alan H. *Egyptian Grammar*. New York: Oxford University Press, 1957.

Gimbutas, Marija. *The Prehistory of Eastern Europe*. Part I (Mesolithic, Neolithic and Copper Age Cultures in Russia and the Baltic Area), Hugh Hencken, ed. Cambridge, Mass.: Peabody Museum, 1956.

Harris, J.R. *Egyptian Art*. Middlesex, England: Spring Books, 1966.

Hassan, Selim. *The Sphinx, Its History in the Light of Recent Excavations*. Cairo: Government Press, 1949.

134

Herodotus, Book II. In *The History of Herodotus,* George Rawlinson, tr., Manuel Komroff, ed. New York: Tudor Publishing Co., 1956.

Josephus, Book I. In *The Works of Flavius Josephus,* William Whiston, tr. Philadelphia: David McKay, Publisher, n.d.

Jung, Carl G. *Man and His Symbols.* Garden City, N.Y.: Doubleday & Co., Inc., 1964.

Leake, Chauncey D. *The Old Egyptian Medical Papyri.* Lawrence, Kans.: University of Kansas Press, 1952.

Lucas, A., ed. *Ancient Egyptian Materials and Industries.* 4th ed. rev. by J.R. Harris. New York: St. Martin's Press, 1962.

Mercer, Samuel A.B. *The Pyramid Texts: In Translation and Commentary.* 2 vols. New York: Longmans, Green and Co., 1952.

Moret, Alexandre. *The Nile and Egyptian Civilization,* M.R. Dobie, tr. New York: Alfred A. Knopf, 1928.

Murray, Margaret A. *The Splendor That Was Egypt.* New & rev. ed. New York: Hawthorn Books, Inc., 1963.

Petrie, Sir (Wm.) Flinders. *A History of Egypt.* 6 vols. New York: Charles Scribner's Sons, 1924.

———. *The Pyramids and Temples of Giza.* London: Field & Tuer, 1883.

———. *Religion and Conscience in Ancient Egypt.* New York: Charles Scribner's Sons, 1898.

Pliny, Book I. In *Natural History,* Paul Turner, ed. Carbondale, Ill.: Southern Illinois University Press, 1962.

Porter, Bertha, and Moss, Rosalind. *Topographical Bibliography of Ancient Egyptian Hieroglyphic Texts, Reliefs and Paintings.* 2nd ed. Oxford, England: Clarendon Press, 1960.

Reisner, George Andrew. *A History of the Giza Necropolis.* Vol. II (The Tomb of Hetep-heres, the Mother of Cheops), comp. and rev. by William Stevenson Smith. Cambridge, Mass.: Harvard University Press, 1955.

Smyth, Piazzi. *Our Inheritance in the Great Pyramid.* London: Wm. Isbister, Ltd., 1880.

Stecchini, Livio Catullo. "Notes on the Relation of Ancient Measures to the Great Pyramid." Appendix to Peter Tompkins' *Secrets of the Great Pyramid,* pp. 289-382. (See following listing.)

Tompkins, Peter. *Secrets of the Great Pyramid.* New York: Harper and Row, 1971.

Trigger, Bruce G. *History and Settlement in Lower Nubia.* New Haven, Conn.: Yale University (publications in anthropology, no. 69), 1965.

Wainwright, Gerald A. *The Sky Religion in Egypt: Its Antiquity and Effects.* Westport, Conn.: Greenwood Press, Publishers, 1971.

THE EDGAR CAYCE LEGACIES

Among the vast resources which have grown out of the late Edgar Cayce's work are:

The Readings: Available for examination and study at the Association for Research and Enlightenment, Inc.,(A.R.E.®) at Virginia Beach, Va., are 14,256 readings consisting of 49,135 pages of verbatim psychic material plus related correspondence. The readings are the clairvoyant discourses given by Cayce while he was in a self-induced hypnotic sleep-state. These discourses were recorded in shorthand and then typed. Copious indexing and cross-indexing make the readings readily accessible for study.

Research and Information: Medical information which flowed through Cayce is being researched and applied by the research divisions of the Edgar Cayce Foundation. Work is also being done with dreams and other aspects of ESP. Much information is disseminated through the A.R.E. Press publications, *A.R.E. News* and *The A.R.E. Journal.* Coordination of a nationwide program of lectures and conferences is in the hands of the Department of Education. A library specializing in psychic literature is available to the public with books on loan to members. An extensive tape library has A.R.E. lectures available for purchase. Resource material has been made available for authors, resulting in the publication of scores of books, booklets and other material.

A.R.E. Study Groups: The Edgar Cayce material is most valuable when worked with in an A.R.E. Study Group, the text for which is *A Search for God,* Books I and II. These books are the outcome of eleven years of work by Edgar Cayce with the first A.R.E. group and represent the distillation of wisdom which flowed through him in the trance condition. Hundreds of A.R.E. groups flourish throughout the United States and other countries. Their primary purpose is to assist the members to know their relationship to their Creator and to become channels of love and service to others. The groups are nondenominational and avoid ritual and dogma. There are no dues or fees required to join a group although contributions may be accepted.

Membership: A.R.E. has an open-membership policy which offers attractive benefits.

For more information write A.R.E., Box 595, Virginia Beach, Va. 23451. To obtain information about publications, please direct your query to A.R.E. Press. To obtain information about joining or perhaps starting an A.R.E. Study Group, please direct your letter to the Study Group Department.